This book is the scanned reproduction of the original edition. It may have occasional imperfections such as blurred type, markings, etc., that were either part of the original copy, or caused by the scanning process.

———————

This edition is reprinted by STAS Editions
with the gracious permission of the Congregation of the Sacred Hearts.

STAS EDITIONS, 2013
21077 Quarry Hill Rd.
Winona, Minnesota 55987

Paperback edition
ISBN 978-1-939409-01-0

On the cover: "The Good Shepherd," by Zefir Kukushev.

PRIESTS

"Shepherds after My own Heart"
(Jeremiah 3:15)

Spiritual Conferences

FATHER MATEO CRAWLEY-BOEVEY, SS.CC.

Translated from the French by
Father Francis Larkin, SS.CC.

Nihil obstat: William Davis, SS.CC.
Imprimi potest: William J. Condon, SS.CC.
                  Provincial
Nihil obstat: Edward A. Cerny, SS., S.T.D.
                  Censor librorum
Imprimatur: Francis P. Keough, D.D.
                  Archbishop of Baltimore

Foreword

I have always considered it one of the special graces of my life to have known Father Mateo. This foreword is written with a deep feeling of gratitude to Almighty God for the gift of a life like that of Father Mateo and for the incalculable influence for good which his apostolate has exercised over many years.

Father Mateo has been called the Apostle of the Enthronement of the Sacred Heart. And this indeed he is, pre-eminently so. He is also in a most special way the Apostle of priestly sanctity, a theme which he was bidden to preach to his fellow priests by the Holy Father himself. Some of the fruits of that preaching will be found in this precious volume.

Father Mateo seems to have made his own the special mission of St. Therese of the Child Jesus, to eliminate the erroneous idea concerning the extraordinary character of sanctity, and to show that sanctity does not demand that one's life be in any way out of the ordinary, but that the common ordinary life of the average good Christian can lead to the highest sanctity, provided it is transformed into an act of the love of God. This teaching he applied with special emphasis to the life of the priest.

Here he had one great consuming passion: to convince every priest that priestly holiness and priestly zeal are in direct proportion to the most sublime act of the priestly life, the celebration of the Holy Sacrifice of the Mass. *Qualis Missa, talis Sacerdos et Apostolus* was the inscription which he invariably wrote on pictures of the Sacred Heart that he would distribute to priests at the retreats which he preached to them. Here is the ''master-idea'' of the preaching of Father Mateo, it seems to me. Ardently promoting the cause of the Sacred Heart in every possible way, he would constantly point to the Mass as the perfect means of being transformed into Christ. In the Mass Father Mateo finds the best means of promoting the truth that sanctity is for everyone, and that it is within the reach of the ordinary person, and that the door is open to all who observe nothing singular in their lives.

One other comment needs to be made. Father Mateo throughout his entire life has vigorously combated every form of Jansenism. His preaching of confidence and trust, based on the solid and orthodox doctrine of the Church concerning devotion to the Sacred Heart of Jesus and to the Immaculate Heart of Mary, was always an outstanding part of the retreats, triduums, and sermons which he gave to priests, religious and lay people alike. Where the love of the Sacred Heart burns in the heart, no amount of suffering, no amount of the magnitude of evil, can rob the heart of the confident joy in the ultimate triumph of that love. Father Mateo insisted that priests need much encouragement in their work, especially in trying to save souls despite themselves. He constantly pointed to the true doctrine of the Sacred Heart as the unfailing source of encouragement in that confident joy which can come only from living in the Heart of Jesus.

While the printed pages of this little volume cannot bring to life the extraordinary gift for moving men which vibrated in every word and gesture of Father Mateo's sermons, it is my sincere hope that many priests will capture something of his enthusiasm and will be kindled with a spark of the great fire which burned in his heart as he delivered these talks with all the ardor of his own priestly heart, and thus be brought closer to the perfection of the priestly Heart of Jesus Himself.

Albert Cardinal Meyer
Archbishop of Chicago

Letter of Pope Pius XII to Father Mateo

From the Vatican,
June 13, 1956

SECRETARIATE OF STATE
OF HIS HOLINESS

No. 377195

Reverend Father:

The International Headquarters of the Work of the Enthronement recently published the text of the *Sacerdotal Retreat* which you preached twenty years ago to French missionaries in Japan. In your name, a copy of this work was presented to the Sovereign Pontiff who received this homage with lively satisfaction.

Immediately following the Encyclical in which he wished, in a solemn manner, to remind Christians throughout the world of the incomparable place of the cult of the Sacred Heart in Christian life, it is particularly pleasing to the head of the Church to congratulate and thank the one who, for so many years, and with such tireless zeal, has been the world-wide apostle of this devotion. And what else is this *Sacerdotal Retreat* but an invitation to priests to draw from the Heart of our Lord the secret of their sanctification and of success in their apostolate?

It gives His Holiness great pleasure to grant you the consolation of realizing, in the evening of your life, that your apostolate is so fully in accord with these sublime teachings of the Vicar of Jesus Christ. With a paternal wish that this little volume which you offered him today be spread far and wide and thus carry the echo of your voice to a great many of your brothers in the priesthood, the common Father of all sends you as a pledge of his constant good will, the Apostolic Blessing.

Together with my sincere thanks for the copy of the book which you sent for my personal use, kindly accept the assurance of my sentiments of devotedness in our Lord.

/s/ A. Dell'Acqua
Subst.

Father Mateo Crawley-Boevey, SS.CC.

Note: *Sacerdotal Retreat* referred to in this letter is the English title of the French text from which the present translation was made.

Preface

Father Mateo's name is well-known to most American priests because of the clergy retreats he preached in the United States from 1940 to 1944, and because of the Enthronement of the Sacred Heart and Night Adoration in the Home which he founded. Many priests know him too from reading *Jesus the King of Love*, or from his other writings.

Few priests have influenced family life on a world-wide scale as has this South American Father of the Sacred Hearts. Since 1907, the year he was cured at Paray-le-Monial, where he received a mission directly from the Sacred Heart, he has preached everywhere the "Social Reign of the Sacred Heart through the Enthronement of the Sacred Heart in the Home." We say "everywhere," for the whole world has been his mission field. Untiringly, preaching many times a day, he has brought the message of the merciful love of the Sacred Heart to almost every country in Europe, the Orient, North and South America.

Millions of families have been affected by his earnest sermons or his eloquent writings. In the United States alone, it is estimated that over a million families have had the Sacred Heart of Jesus enthroned in their homes and some 300,000 individuals and families are making Night Adoration in their homes. Given the social influence of religion in the home, the impact on public life of Father Mateo's apostolate for the sanctification of the family can scarcely be over-estimated.

But it is in the field of clergy retreats that Father Mateo has made his greatest contribution to the advancement of the Kingdom of Christ here on earth.

Few, if any, priests have given as many retreats to priests in as many countries as has Father Mateo. In Spanish (his native tongue), French, English, Italian, and Portuguese he has preached the doctrine of priestly sanctity to the clergy (both secular and regular) of almost every nationality. This was especially true when he was invited by many bishops and vicars-apostolic of the Orient to conduct retreats to missionaries from many lands throughout the Far East. From 1935 to 1940, he preached almost unceasingly in Japan, Korea, Manchuria, China, Indochina, Malaya, India, Ceylon, the East Indies, the Philippines and Hawaii. To native priests unfamiliar with European languages he preached full retreats in Latin, no mean feat!

Before leaving Japan, the missionaries urged him to leave with them a summary of the doctrine of priestly holiness which he had preached to them. This he did in a book published in French under the title of *Retraite Sacerdotale*. As the author remarked in his preface: "This book is a summary of my retreat. I say 'summary,' for naturally I had to omit certain conferences and also certain facts of a personal nature, necessary for a retreat but better omitted from a publication, for *scripta manent et. . .volant.*' "

This book was first published in 1936. In 1956, on the occasion of the centenary of the extension of the Feast of the Sacred Heart of the universal Church, it was reprinted and a copy sent in Father Mateo's name to Pope Pius XII. It merited the splendid tribute to the veteran priest found in the letter printed in this volume.

As Father John d'Elbee, SS.CC., former Superior General of the Fathers of the Sacred Hearts, remarked in his preface to the 1956 edition: "A remarkable fact about Father Mateo, the world apostle of the Sacred Heart of Jesus, is the gift which he received from heaven profoundly to move his audiences, whether the masses or the elite, and the 'elite of the elite,' priests.

"In the last years of his life, especially, he preferred to preach to priests. This is quite understandable. 'The priest,' he says, 'is, immediately after Mary, the divine masterpiece of grace, of dignity and power.' He adds, 'Unfortunately this thought does not move us as it should, for we are too accustomed to hearing ourselves called other Christs.'

"The entire book is filled with this supernatural thinking. In these pages will be found the essential principles of the evangelical doctrine preached by Father Mateo, and, we might add, his priestly soul. In them is contained the substance of all he has said and written.

"How many bishops and priests have told us, 'My interior life, in fact my whole life, was transformed as a result of an unforgettable retreat preached by Father Mateo. What a debt of gratitude I owe him!' "

* * * * *

Father Mateo (Edward) Crawley-Boevey, SS.CC., was born on November 18, 1875 in Tingo, near Arequipa, Peru. His father, a member of an aristocratic English family, was a banker, an Anglican, converted when he married a devout Peruvian Catholic of Spanish descent. The family moved to Valparaiso, Chile about 1881. Here Edward studied at the College conducted by the Fathers of the Sacred Hearts, and later became a priest in this Congregation, of which Father Damien was a member. He was appointed professor, and in 1903, director of a school of law which developed into the Catholic University of Valparaiso.

In 1906 an earthquake destroyed the law school, and as a result, Father Mateo's health broke down. Ordered by his doctors to travel in Europe, he went to Rome, where with the help of Cardinals Merry del Val and Vives, he obtained a private audience with Pope St. Pius X. Having explained his plan for enthroning the Sacred Heart in the home, he requested permission to preach it. To his surprise, he was "commanded" to devote his life to this "work of social salvation." Soon, he was in Paray-le-Monial, where on August 24, 1907, he was restored to health upon entering the chapel of apparitions. The same night in "a sudden illumination," he saw clearly that the Enthronement of the Sacred Heart in the home, the social cell, was to be made the basis for a world-wide crusade for the establishing of the "Social Reign of the Sacred Heart of Jesus."

This was the providential beginning of Father Mateo's long career. Often handicapped by infirmities of various kinds, he managed to keep going, claiming that preaching about "the King of Love" was the best possible tonic for him. This has been verified by American priests who heard him preach fiery sermons even though he was 65 when he came to this country. Often, at the opening of a conference, he would be too weak to begin at once. At the end, he was an entirely different man, seemingly transformed by the very fact of talking about the Sacred Heart.

Father Mateo's active career came to an end in 1946 while preaching in Canada. Forced into a hospital ("the Sacred Heart never consulted me about this!") by a serious ailment, he remained a patient until February, 1956, when he recovered sufficiently (and unexpectedly) to fly back to Valparaiso. During these long years, he was very active with his pen, having many articles published in various languages. Among these are *The Holy Sacrifice of the Mass* (National Enthronement Center, Fairhaven, Mass. 02719); and *Bethany of the Sacred Heart* (chapter fifteen of this book).

* * * * *

The present volume was translated from the French. This was no easy task, for Father Mateo has a style peculiar to himself. The translator has endeavored to retain the smoothness of the original French, while keeping in mind the literary tastes of American priests. Whether he has succeeded is quite another matter.

Several conferences not contained in the French edition, but taken from Father Mateo's English notes, have been added. The chapter on the Enthronement, originally published under the title *Bethany of the Sacred*

Heart, was also included, though it was not preached as such.

Francis Larkin, SS.CC.

Note: Father Mateo died on May 4, 1960, in the Sacred Hearts College, Valparaiso, Chile, at the age of eighty-five. The concluding words of his last article, "On Priestly Vocations," are significant: "The Lord is my witness that my only desire is to transform my last days into a thrice-holy Mass, and thus be consumed slowly for Him, the Victim, Mediator and Pontiff, and through this immolation of love to glorify the Blessed Trinity by redeeming many priestly souls, Thy Kingdom Come!" In his spiritual testament he requested that after his death Masses be offered, not for him, but for the Reign of the Sacred Heart for his intentions. "In this way," he said, *"defunctus adhuc loquitur."*

On the occasion of his death, His Holiness, Pope John XXIII, sent the following letter to the Superior General of the Fathers of the Sacred Hearts:

Segretaria de Stato
di Sua Santita

li 16 Mai, 1960
Dal Vaticano

Very Reverend Father:

His Holiness received your recent letter in which you apprised him of the death of Father Mateo Crawley-Boevey. He wishes me to transmit to you his paternal and heartfelt condolences and to assure you of his prayers for the repose of the soul of this illustrious religious. The Holy Father is quite familiar with the role played by Father Mateo in the diffusion of the cult of the Sacred Heart, whose tireless apostle he had been during his entire life. Moreover he is pleased to think that the sad loss sustained by your religious family will be compensated by the presence in Heaven — it is permitted to believe this — of a new and powerful protector.

The Holy Father was also edified by the attitude manifested by the regretted deceased in his last hours. He has no doubt that your Congregation, following the example of Father Mateo, will continue to labor for the greater glory of the Sacred Heart. For this intention he most willingly imparts to you and to all the members of your Institute, a special Apostolic Blessing.

Kindly accept, Reverend Father, the assurance of my devotion in our Lord.

†A. Dell'Acqua
Subst.

After Father Mateo's death in 1960, the following letter was found among his papers. It was in his handwriting and without date. FATHER MATEO SPEAKS TO PRIESTS was published, for the first time, shortly after his death. He was aware of the forthcoming publication and had planned to send this letter to the translator. We feel its publication in this new edition of his conferences is timely. In his "Last Will and Testament" (cf. appendix) he wrote, "Even from my tomb I must continue to preach the sovereignty of love and mercy of the Heart of Jesus." We trust this re-publication of these conferences for priests will enable him to carry out his last wish. (TR)

Colegio de los Sagrados Corazones
Valparaiso, Chile

Dear Father Larkin:

Words spoken for the glory of the Lord Jesus are eminently apostolic, hence not limited to any one country. Rather, they are universal, catholic in scope. This is the case of the Gospel. Written in Hebrew or Aramaic, the Good Tidings have been translated into every known language and dialect, for the salvation of all men.

Beloved confrere, Father Larkin, in an apostolic spirit and for the spiritual profit of the American clergy you have had the extreme kindness of translating into English my sacerdotal retreat preached in Japan and in many other countries.

As recompense, may the Sacred Heart of Jesus bless you! As for me, I thank you for having given me this opportunity to again share in your magnificent apostolate in your beloved country, far greater because of its religious spirit than politically and financially — and that is saying a great deal. I say this not to please American readers, but rather because of conviction, for I have a deep knowledge of America. Despite inevitable short-comings, your people by their marvelous generosity and powerful means of communication have become an instrument of Divine Providence and a splendid messenger of the Church and the Gospel.

In this great evangelical mission the clergy can, and must, play a preponderant and decisive role. This means that the clergy, the elite, *par excellence*, of a country, must be penetrated, by grace and prayer, with a supernatural spirit. These conferences which you are publishing will, I hope, be for them a pleasing and strengthening food.

Let me add that I am praying for the success of this little volume for reasons of gratitude. For the United States received me, South American that I am, as though I were a pure-blooded "Yankee." Thanks to this cordial welcome, I was able to travel far and wide with as much success as fatigue for the glory and the reign of the Heart of Jesus, the King of Love. May He be blessed a thousand times for it! May He water with His Blood the seed sowed in His name for the one sole purpose of presenting to Him a crown made up of priestly souls, truly men of prayer!

Father Mateo Crawley-Boevey, SS.CC.

Contents

Spiritual Conferences for

PRIESTS

Your friends have been exceedingly honored,
O God. . . .Be saints.

1. Priestly Perfection

The masterpiece of moral creation and of the omnipotence and the love of God was without doubt the Immaculate Virgin. She stands apart, unique. The uncreated beauty of our Lord poured into her soul the goodness and grandeur of God as far as they can be reproduced in a mere creature. "Thou art all-fair. O Mary!"

But immediately after Mary comes the priest, the divine masterpiece of grace, of dignity and of power.

Unfortunately this thought does not move us as it should, for we are too accustomed to hearing ourselves called *Alter Christus.* Yet this title is far from being a merely conventional one, like so many worldly titles. On the contrary, it corresponds to a divine reality, for we are in truth *Christs.* As one Father of the Church puts it, "The priest is something midway between a human and divine nature!" St. Clement goes even further when he calls the priest: "After God, an earthly God." This would seem to be an exaggeration were it not for the fact that it has as its doctrinal basis the sacerdotal character itself and, as an overwhelming argument, our priestly powers.

The altar and confessional leave no room for error or even for exaggeration, for the powers of consecration and absolution infinitely surpass all created powers. I have no trouble understanding the reason for the astonishment of the Jews when they heard Jesus saying to the paralytic,

"Rise, thy sins are forgiven thee." They were perfectly right in arguing, "Who can speak thus without blaspheming, except God alone?" No one save God can pronounce the sacred formula which we ourselves use in the confessional, without blaspheming.

We can go even further: at the altar we command our Lord Himself and He obeys.

This brings to mind another cause of scandal for the Jews and even for some of the disciples: at Capharnaum Jesus declared He would give His flesh as food and His blood as drink. Imagine their reaction had they even remotely suspected the undreamed of miraculous privilege of our daily Mass! In truth the priest is "an earthly God, after God — Thy friends have been exceedingly honored, O God!"

But even in the priesthood there is a scale of values. Take, for example, the case of the first apostles. Even though our priesthood is the same as theirs, still it seems quite evident they received greater marks of our Lord's trust than we, for friendship is measured by the amount of trust placed in one's friends.

The apostles, however, were the advance guard and the pioneers of the message of redemption; they were the first ambassadors of the Great King. By the very fact that they were first in honor, they were first in dangers, the first to receive the violent reaction of the pagan society they were trying to conquer. They fulfilled their privileged role as objects of the opposition and hatred of the pagans very well: of the twelve apostles, eleven were martyrs.

* * * * *

Everything I have just said, consoling because true, is merely the introduction to a lesson I now wish to point out for the greater glory of the Sacred Heart of Jesus.

Reasoning simply but doctrinally, I assert that to such supernatural dignity of character, of power and of mission, must correspond an equal depth of interior life, of priestly holiness. If then, by the power and the mission conferred upon me, I am truly an *Alter Christus*, I must also be one by my mode of life. Otherwise, if I were permitted to be simply an upright man, an ecclesiastical functionary, and not a saint, then God for the first time would have made a monstrosity. He would have upset the balance of the priesthood: there would be a chasm between our virtue and our power. In this hypothesis, the priest would be of heaven because of his sacerdotal character, and of this earth because of a perfectly legitimate easygoing life of mediocrity. Such want of equilibrium never has been and never could be the work of the Lord.

Hence, He who made me a priest must necessarily have willed to give me, together with my ordination, all the means I need to become a true priest, a well-balanced priest in the full sense of the word.

A Christ who works miracles of grace, but who is not a miracle of grace himself, is not the authentic Christ God wants him to be.

I will now sum up all our dignity and all our power as priests in the celebration of the Holy Sacrifice of the Mass. And I affirm: if Holy Mass is a divine reality — the most divine of all realities — if I really have the power of transubstantiation, of officially offering to the Father the divine Victim, through Christ, with Christ, and in Christ, then it necessarily follows that such a marvelous and divine sacrifice must in itself have the power to sanctify me. To have the power to offer Mass, and not to have the means nor the duty to become a saintly priest are ideas and terms which are mutually exclusive. Therefore, *because I officially offer the Holy Sacrifice, I must be a real saint!*

* * * * *

To what has already been said, we can add the argument of our mission, of our calling. The wisdom, the justice, the love of God which have launched us on a sea full of the gravest responsibilities, must necessarily have given us more than we need to carry out our redemptive mission.

But note well, this mission of ours does not consist alone or principally in the necessary parish or church administration, but rather in the solid, supernatural, spiritual life of the priest. Moreover, this deep, interior holiness of life will be the soul of all our activities, and will prevent us from becoming mere ecclesiastical functionaries.

Mary, Joseph, and John the Baptist had to be spiritual giants because of their lofty mission, and this strict rule also applies to us. You have never seen and you never will see the "miracle in reverse" of someone to whom our Lord has confided a certain mission, but of whom He has not simultaneously demanded corresponding holiness. Thus we can affirm that the measure of the greatness of a mission is always the yardstick of the degree of sanctity God requires of him whom He has appointed as His messenger.

Let us be frank and admit that we have not insisted enough on this fundamental principle. We can even say that sometimes in the formation of priests there has been a certain tacit approval of the idea that a minimum of spiritual formation was sufficent. We are reminded of the story of Gideon: one would say that more hope has been placed in 3,000 professional soldiers than in the grace that sustained 300 picked, hardened men.

There seems to be a fear of asking too much, when in fact it is simply a question of demanding what a priest is obliged to give in justice and out of love. On the other hand, there has not been enough fear of the thousand times more harmful plague of priestly mediocrity. Let us uphold with honor the traditions of our priesthood. Do not stay on the ground: rise high on the wings of great desires; work hard to become saints; fear one thing only: mediocrity!

Often think over these words: "Sancti estote. . . . Estote perfecti. . . ." (Lev. 11:14) Keep in mind, as Dom Marmion tells us, that this command does not merely announce the law of salvation, but rather the law of holiness. If these words are not applicable to us priests, consecrated men, when and where and to whom will they be applicable? It would be incredible if they were meant for a Thérèse of Lisieux and not for an *Alter Christus!*

One final thought: Everyone knows that not all forms of the sacred ministry are practical for all regions, for all parishes, or even for all priests. I know of only one form of work that is suitable to all places and to all priests, and which must everywhere and always be the foundation of all apostolic works whatever they may be, and that is *priestly holiness!*

Whether you are bowed down under the yoke of fatigue and old age at 80, or broken by sickness at 35, have one dominant ambition at all times: to present to the Master of the harvest a priestly heart burning with a desire to love Him as only the saints know how to love. Believe me, a priestly heart on fire with love will make up a thousand times over for what is lacking in your external ministry and will result in some very great surprises for you when you stand before the tribunal of God. This is the *unum necessarium* — the *only* possible thing God will demand from you.

St. Pius X was right in saying — for Rome and for the Missions — "Those who are obliged to form Jesus Christ in the souls of their brothers, must have first formed Him in their own souls, thereby becoming Christs and making the words of St. Paul a reality: *'mihi vivere Christus est.'* " (Phil. 1:21).

* * * * *

If you are obliged to become a saintly priest, then your first duty is to have an intense desire to do so. During your thanksgiving, renew the sincere, manly desires for priestly perfection: to advance each day toward the summit of holiness, even though it be but one step. Never forget that in the eyes of God, who sees everything, sincere, loyal, burning desires are already an act of genuine love. Recall the words of St. Francis de Sales: "To want to love is to love."

Grace will never be lacking, for by virtue of your priesthood and your Mass you receive it in abundance, and it will be superabundant to the degree that you draw it down in torrents by the greatness of your desires.

With a manly will, then, make every effort to go higher, for He who has called you to the priesthood and the apostolate has also called you to sanctity: "Put out into the deep" (Luke 5:4). He who is able to celebrate Mass and to save souls for eternity, can — and must — certainly become a real saint.

But once more, you must will it with a sincere, manly, and priestly will!

Heart of Jesus, burning with love for me,
inflame my heart with love for Thee!

I am the way (John 14:6).

2. The Simplicity of Sanctity

To enunciate and lay down principles is not enough; it is also necessary to smooth the path for their application, to give courage, and to show how to put them into practice. That is the purpose of this conference.

The theme of the previous chapter was that the dignity of the priesthood demands of priests and future priests nothing less than *sanctity*. I know many priests who admit this principle theoretically, but in practice live lives of discouragement of indifference as far as its application to their daily lives is concerned.

I would like to confirm this fundamental principle by showing, not necessarily the *facility*, but the *perfect simplicity* of the means that God wishes us to use in sanctifying ourselves in what I like to call the *royal road of daily duty*.

I repeat, if by reason of my great dignity, and because of my lofty mission I am obliged to tend toward perfection and strive to become a saint, I certainly must be able to do this, for there is no such thing as a duty impossible of fulfillment. I have my defects and my weaknesses; but if I am a priest and can say Mass, then I have all I need to be a saint. "To think the contrary," says Dom Marmion, "would be a doctrinal error and a sin of timidity inexcusable in a priest."

What road is to be followed? What providential route has been mapped out for the priest to help him to reach these spiritual heights? In other words, how may we become saints without ever leaving the place where God wills us to be? The road to sanctity is not necessarily the road to the nearest Trappist monastery! Listen to this doctrinal answer given by Cardinal Mercier, speaking with personal authority: *"By living your priesthood fully."* He adds: "We do not believe enough in the power of the grace of our priestly character. . . .

"The grace of the priesthood," he continues, "is in itself so powerful and so efficacious, that without anything else the truly faithful priest can become a man of God, a saint." In truth, the sacrament of holy orders which raises me to the unique dignity of Christ, should be able to realize in me what this dignity demands of me. And the very first requirement is that I be, not a mere likeness of Christ, not a watered down Christ, but a Christ whole and entire, an integral Christ.

Thus in virtue of the *ex opere operato*, the sacrament of holy orders confers upon me, together with the character and priestly powers, sufficient grace to enable me to live up to my lofty dignity, that is, to sanctify me. It follows that it is the *ex opere operantis* which has to fructify and develop in me the germ of priestly sanctity planted by the sacrament of holy orders.

Never forget that according to our Lord's plan, our sublime dignity does not consist exclusively in the priestly character, but in what this character demands as its accidental and moral complement, namely our personal and supernatural perfection, the *living* of our priesthood to the full! In this sense — which is the only true one — we can state and affirm that *ordination is always an official and solemn call to that sanctity* without which our priesthood remains in part inefficacious. It clearly follows that the Master who calls me to holiness of life offers me in the sacrament itself the necessary grace to accomplish fully His Will. I have a right to this grace, because of the wisdom, the justice and the love of Christ, who wills that I be a one hundred per cent priest! And He who owes it to me wants this grace to be rich and superabundant, for He knows — with sorrow — that by my lack of holiness I could waste the treasures of my priesthood, and that it could even be a crushing weight for me and sterile in giving supernatural life to souls.

· It was because of this doctrine that St. Ephrem could state: "The priest is a stupendous miracle, with unspeakable power; he touches heaven, mingles with the angels, and is on familiar terms with God."

May we always have an unbounded and lively faith in the marvelous grace of our priesthood!

* * * * *

And now, to be practical, a few encouraging and solid considerations regarding our great duty to sanctify ourselves. How best utilize the grace of our priesthood in order to reach that fullness of divine life that we call priestly holiness? In the first place, the very exercise of our sublime ministry should be, according to God's plan, a means of sanctifying the priest: *to give God is always to enrich oneself with God!*

As a matter of fact, in justice, the first grace of the apostolate is always for the apostle. Thus, whether you preach or whether you distribute Holy Communion, Jesus whom you give to your people, gives Himself to you in return a hundred, a thousand times over as a reward for having given Him to others, provided of course you give Him with the proper dispositions.

Was not this the case of Mary, who became richer with Jesus when she gave us Jesus? Yes, she was richer on the first Christmas day than she was on the 25th of March and still richer with Jesus when she gave Him to us on Calvary's heights.

The same is true for us: everything you do for your flock — administration of the sacraments, preaching, various activities, everything without exception, is a tremendous treasure of sanctifying grace for you, first of all, the docile instruments. But this is true only when an indispensable condition is fulfilled, namely that we be *priests* and always remain *priests* and never become machines or simple ecclesiastical functionaries.

There is no doubt about it; there exists a tacit contract between the Master of the vineyard and us the vinedressers, His official representatives. It is this: that the firstfruits and also a high percentage of the income belong to those who are in charge of the administration of His vineyard. St. Paul expressed the same truth in another way: "They who serve the altar, have their share with the altar" (I Cor. 9:13). If this was said of a well-merited material offering, it is a thousand times more true when taken in the spiritual sense of compensations and rewards for the services rendered to our Lord through our work for souls: "You did it for me" (Matt. 25:40).

Have we not always been told that charity to the poor comes back to the benefactor a hundred times over? Then what are we to say of that other more perfect kind of charity which the priest gives to souls and often to the most neglected souls? Why is it that this beautiful and consoling doctrine is not more insisted upon? Why, when speaking of apostolic work, do we stress the dignity of the apostle and his reward in heaven as well as the benefits he confers upon souls, and so seldom the reward given here below to the apostle himself? We should often remind ourselves of the story of Christ appearing to St. Martin, clothed in the cloak given by the saint to a beggar a short time before.

If I have already told you, *"Be saints to be apostles,"* I now wish to add, *"Be apostles to be saints."*

* * * * *

Now we come to one of the most consoling principles of spiritual life and of our priestly life. It is this: the realization that we can become saints — saints with a capital "S" — in the quite simple, normal path of the performance of our daily duties. On the foundation of a solid interior life, a life of faith and prayer, the second element of sanctification is our daily life lived in all the beauty, the simplicity, and the monotony of Nazareth, and this in the place assigned to us by divine Providence. Without changing or adding anything to our program of daily duties — unless it be the addition of a strong faith and an intense love — all of us must and can become genuine saints.

I agree with Dom Marmion that there are ". . .some people so narrow-minded that they are scandalized at the simplicity of this divine plan." They are the same ones who often confuse the *mission* of the saint with his *life*, and who cannot think of sanctity without the "fireworks" of miracles and the halo of charisms. They seem to forget that nothing was wanting to the sanctity of Mary at Nazareth, and yet her holiness was without ecstasies or marvels. She, the only perfect saint, was certainly the humblest and the simplest of creatures, living her life in the background and shadows, doing the will of God in an astounding way. *On the other hand, Judas probably worked miracles, but is far from being a saint!*

The will of God is sanctifying in itself, if only we knew how to accept it and fulfill it. This is true especially of the two phases of the pattern of our daily life. The first phase consists of the duties of our priestly state. For us they are well defined. We must not perform them like soldiers or pagans, stoically, or fatalistically; but with love, love for the Crucified.

Then there *are the thousand and one crosses*, big and small, which are an integral part of our state of life. I call these the "classical penances" of the life Jesus has willed for each one of us. Here is a type of mortification for priests a thousand times better than hair-shirts or fastings, one whose irritations and sharp points can make of us great penitents. If you perform no other kind of penances than those which our Lord sends you each day, and accept them with love, believe me, before God the mortified monks of the pentitential orders will have no greater merit than you.

Have a great love for the thrice holy cross of your priestly state. Don't drag that cross. Certainly it is a heavy one, but like the heavy wings of huge planes, this weighty cross should be for you a means of getting off the ground and soaring aloft.

There can be no sanctity without penance. But in the chalice of suffering of every priest, Jesus has placed just

31

enough providential penance to supply this need and to make of him a holy priest and a successful apostle.

* * * * *

It is a good idea to go back frequently and meditate on the incomparable lesson Nazareth has for all of us. Here we are taught to follow in the footsteps of Jesus, Mary, and Joseph, the earthly trinity. We do not have to invent anything new to become saints. The path is already laid out for us. It is Jesus Christ Himself who is constantly reminding us: "Come after me. . . .I have given you the example. . . .I am the way."

Keep in mind that the Incarnate Word willed us to live our life to the full, to perfect ours by His, and to identify Himself with it down to its smallest details. He did this precisely in order to simplify and to make possible the realization of our own important duty of Christian and priestly holiness. Since the time of Nazareth, then, nothing is insignificant or trivial in this life. But above all, in the life of a priest, the other Christ, everything is great and everything should be divine and holy, provided that we have a lively faith and a burning love. "All is great where love is great!"

No need to seek the summit of sanctity outside of or away from the altogether simple life led at Nazareth. Here it is to be found in all its marvelous simplicity. Do not dream of finding perfection in another way, but look for it within the framework of your seemingly commonplace life. With some variations, this was the often tiring and rough life led by St. Paul and St. Francis Xavier. *Therein and only therein lies your perfection, because it is the will of God!*

Let us be frank and admit that this is something we have in great part forgotten, little understood and, in general, not sufficiently preached. How many good priests have I not met — well-trained priests in other respects — for whom the preaching of this doctrine has had the appeal of a new discovery or of a genuine novelty. Yes, a novelty, one that dates back to Nazareth, to the

Gospels!

Once more I maintain that it has not been said and resaid often enough that *any priest whatsoever, no matter how ordinary his assignment, who lives his priesthood to the full by giving his whole heart to the Church and to souls, can become a true saint, and in the eyes of God, a big one.* For this only one miracle is required of him, that of a holy daily Mass!

The candidates for the priesthood who come to us have not been sufficiently reminded that they can become holy without the charisms of frightening austerities of the Curé of Ars, and be as holy as he! They have not been told that they can sanctify themselves without the ecstasies during Mass of a St. Bernard or a St. Philip Neri; that they can be real men of God without the extraordinary marvels of a St. Vincent Ferrer or the altogether special way of life of a Charles de Foucauld, or the unusual gifts of a St. Francis Xavier, provided of course they have their great faith and love. The genius is born a genius but the saint is made a saint.

The paths followed by the saints can be, and often are, quite different. But what is common to them all and what makes the saint, is the doing of the will of God, accepting it lovingly whether it is a question of the great and marvelous Teresa of Avila or the no less marvelous Thérèse of Lisieux walking in her "little way" of Nazareth.

I can think of no more solid or appropriate doctrine for priests than that, if they want to steep themselves in the spirit of the Heart of Jesus, and to find in Him new strength to continue climbing the difficult hill of perfection. *"Duc in altum"* (Luke 5:4). It is because we have forgotten much of this that divine Providence, always vigilant and wise, has loudly sounded the powerful warning bell of Lisieux. It seems that heaven has let fall around the Little Flower a vertitable shower of miracles, in order to remind both theologians and little souls of these important truths:

—That it is possible to become a saint in any state of life, by any method, but that the path of simplicity and humility is the surest way of becoming a *big saint,* provided you love with a great deal of love.

—That by *your generous love you can transform* the most insignificant events of daily life.

—*That sanctity does not consist of doing extraordinary things, but in doing the ordinary things with an extraordinary love.*

We have the authoritative words of Pius XI on this subject: "St Thérèse of Lisieux is truly the *Vox Dei*, that will lead consecrated souls, especially priests, her brothers, and missionaries, her privileged friends, to the heights of sanctity by the path of her 'little way,' which is that of Nazareth. Here is a method of sanctifying yourself that is within the reach of every one of you. It is the best, because it is the one followed by Mary and Joseph. It is also the surest, for it does away with illusions and self deception."

The Master is calling you: "Come after Me . . . I have given you the example . . . I am the Way . . . Be perfect!"

* * * * *

Get rid of anything that might be the cause of illusion or discouragement, resolving to sanctify yourself in the perfect fulfillment of your duties. You will find our Lord waiting to accompany you on this road and to give you His graces in abundance.

Sanctify yourself, then, by your daily meditation, regular and frequent confession, and by the devout recitation of your Divine Office.

Sanctify yourself in the exercise of your ministry, often tiring and monotonous, but the one assigned to you by the Church and your superiors.

Sanctify yourself in the joys and sorrows, in the consolations and deceptions that come to every zealous priest.

Sanctify yourself wherever you are, whether healthy or sick, in abundance or in need, encouraged or criticized, always trying to see, to fulfill, and to praise the Will of God.

Sanctify yourself in the thousand and one seemingly insignificant events of daily life, which are a hidden treasure for us priests.

Above all, become a saint through the fervent and careful celebration of the Holy Sacrifice of the Mass, and sanctify yourself to offer it less unworthily.

Have courage! Keep climbing higher and higher, following in the footsteps of Jesus, Mary and Joseph, remembering that all is great where faith is great, but especially that *all is great and divine where love is great and where love is burning!*

He chose for Himself a priest
to offer to Him a sacrifice of praise.

3. Holy Mass, the Means of Priestly Holiness

I consider the subject of the Holy Sacrifice of the Mass so important that before beginning I should like to offer a prayer in union with the Queen of the clergy, that my heart and my pen will be less unworthy to write on such a great mystery of faith and love.

"Glory to the Father, in thanksgiving for the wonderful gift of the Word, His Son, in the Mystery of the Incarnation!

"Glory to the Son of God, the Lamb, in thanksgiving for the mystery of the Redemption through the shedding of His Blood on the cross.

"Glory to the Paraclete, the Spirit of Truth and substantial Love, in thanksgiving for the incomparable gift of the priesthood, by virtue of which we go to the altar and offer the Father the spotless Victim.

"Glory, praise, and love to the three adorable Persons of the Blessed Trinity, *per Christum Dominum Nostrum*, the Mediator and Victim in the Holy Sacrifice of the Mass."

* * * * *

According to God's plan, Holy Mass should daily accomplish two miracles, that of transubstantiation, and that of the sanctification of the celebrant, which are, or ought to be, the corallaries and the firstfruits of his Mass. The first of these two marvels is always and infallibly brought about in every Mass; the second, sad to say, suffers many exceptions.

If the host and the chalice could speak, how often would they not say to the celebrant: "At your priestly word the substance of bread and wine have disappeared; we retain only their accidents, their appearances; we have become 'The Christ, the Son of the living God.' And you, priest-consecrator, when will you work this miracle of love in yourself? When will you have at the altar and in your ministry by the virtue and grace of the Mass, only the appearance of a man, having become in reality an *Alter Christus?*"

In giving Himself up to us under the appearances of bread, our Lord wished to consume us while allowing us to consume Him. To consume Him is easy, for that is why He gives Himself to us. But to allow ourselves to be consumed by Him and with Him in the fire of the divine sacrifice, that is, to be transformed into Jesus, supposes on the part of the celebrant a generous and total oblation that the Heart of Jesus unfortunately does not always find.

We shall give ourselves up to His love when instead of merely pronouncing through routine the sacred words which sum up all the power and dignity of the Holy Sacrifice, *"Through Him, with Him, in Him,. . .all glory and honor is Yours, Almighty Father. . . ,"* we say them from the bottom of our hearts and really try to live them. When each one of us has become a "celebrant and victim" together with Jesus Christ, only then will our Mass be in reality the all-powerful source of sanctifying grace for us priests, of redemption for our people, and the best possible hymn of praise and glory to the Blessed Trinity.

A priest may have many outstanding qualities, but if he has not grasped the tremendous meaning of His Mass in relation to his priesthood and to his spiritual life, he is far from the ideal willed by God. In this regard I like to recall the story related to me by the great Dom Chautard, former Cistercian abbot and author of *The Soul of the Apostolate*. He and two companions were returning from a Eucharistic Congress. As they were taking a shortcut to their monastery they approached the home of a peasant, before which a small boy was playing. When the boy saw the three monks approaching, he ran toward his house shouting, "Come quickly, mother, *three Masses* are coming down the road!"

The learned Dom Chautard turned to the two priests and remarked: "Fathers, of all the discourses on the priesthood we heard at the Congress, that is the best of all!"

As Cardinal Mercier tells us, "Any priest who has understood the sublimity of his Mass, and who seriously tries to make it the center and the divine source of his priestly life, such a one at death will be capable of being canonized!"

How many priests there are who waste the rich treasures of their priesthood, simply because they consider their Mass as just one of a number of priestly functions, instead of making it the most important of their priestly duties so that their entire priesthood graviates around the altar! *We are priests to celebrate the Holy Sacrifice.*

In this connection, listen to this excerpt from a conference given by a Bishop at Lourdes during a Priests' Congress: "Sometimes you think the priest is above all the man of the Gospels and of apostolic activities, and that the best priest is the one who devotes himself entirely to various apostolic movements. Some there are who think the very essence of the priesthood is the care of souls. No! The priest is before and above all the quasi-divine man of the Mass, the one who offers sacrifice. The Mass is his specialty, he is the Mass, and he is fully a priest only at the altar. As it is the happiness of Jesus the adorable Victim to find His priest at the altar, so it should be the joy of the priest to find Jesus the divine Victim in the Mass."

It is a truly divine vocation that places us almost on the same level as Jesus Christ as mediators and victims when we celebrate the "great action," as the Mass was once called.

* * * * *

And now I ask our Lady to enlighten me and bless me, for I should like to present her as the ideal of the priest offering sacrifice and deeply penetrated with the meaning of the action he performs.

There are three mysteries in the life of Mary in which she is represented as fulfilling a sort of priestly function, of which our Mass seems to be a mystical reproduction.

"Et incarnatus est de Spiritu Sancto ex Maria Virgine." When Mary became the mother of the Incarnate Word, was not her first act to offer to the Father the One He had confided to her? And is not this precisely what every priest does each morning, on the paten of the Heart of Mary, as he renews Mary's offering made the very day of the Incarnation? The divine oblation and its ends were the same on that 25th of March at Nazareth as they are every morning on our altar. Would that Mary would share with us the splendor of her purity, the beauty of her humility, the intensity of her love, in order that we might celebrate Holy Mass with these dispositions of priestly holiness!

But this first oblation was made in secret, in the privacy of her soul, and so it had to be made outwardly, sacramentally, if I may use the expression. Thus it was that "according to the law of Moses, they took him up to Jerusalem to present him to the Lord" (Luke 2:22). There Mary Immaculate offered the spotless Lamb in the Temple to the Father, for the glory and salvation of His people. Our Lady is Mother of the Messias only that she might cooperate in His redemptive mission and offer Him for the glory of Him who had sent Him. Through Mary's intercession may our daily Mass please the Father as did the oblation of the Child Jesus in the Temple, when He was presented to the Father through the hands of His most Holy Mother.

Finally we come to Calvary. "He was offered because it was His own will" (Isa. 53:7). At the side of the Victim "stood the Mother," renewing the offering she made on the day of the Incarnation and of the Presentation in the

39

Temple. For if Jesus delivers Himself up through love, so also Mary, with the full right of her divine motherhood, delivers Him up to the Father through love, mingling her bitter tears with His Most Precious Blood.

As you well know, our chalice of the New Covenant renews this mystery of blood in an unbloody manner. As on Calvary, so also at the solemn moment of our Mass, we need Mary to strengthen us and above all to inflame our hearts!

Ask the ''Mother of priests'' for the supreme grace of being delivered once and for all from the terrible evil of the sin of routine in the celebration of the mystery of the Holy Sacrifice of the Mass.

* * * * *

At this point I should like to stress certain dispositions or prerequisites necessary for priests who wish to draw abundant fruit from the fervent celebration of the Holy Sacrifice.

Above all else make a careful preparation for Mass. Despite your overload of work and despite the unforeseen tasks added to your daily program, make an effort to prepare your Mass well. If you habitually neglect this preparation, you run the risk of wasting in part at least the extraordinary grace of your Mass. Get up early enough to prepare your Mass. To do this, go to bed as early as you can; this is the meaning of the expression, ''Go to bed early and save your soul!'' Never go from your bed to the altar. If through no fault of your own you have five minutes to pray before Mass, use four of them as preparation. I recommend the prayerful reading of the Canon of the Mass or the entire Mass of the day as one of the best and most priestly preparations for Holy Mass.

Ask our Blessed Mother to help you in this preparation by communicating to you her spirit of prayer and the dispositions of her Heart on Good Friday, while a few feet away, under her very eyes, they nailed to the cross her child and her God.

Next, celebrate your Mass with great piety, having no other thought or preoccupation than that of glorifying the

Blessed Trinity, who at this moment receive through Jesus Christ the most perfect homage possible, the only one worthy of the divine Majesty. When I say "with great piety," I mean to accentuate the great simplicity and the intensity of faith and love which this "great action" demands of the celebrant, at this sacred moment more than ever a Christ. We should be penetrated with the greatness of this mystery, as though for an instant the veil were lifted and we saw what John saw on Mount Tabor and on Calvary: the majesty of the glorified Christ and the crucified Christ, the two mysteries that are combined at the altar.

Sometimes our Lord does "lift the veil" to strengthen our faith, and allows us to see that the Mass is indeed Calvary surrounded by the glory of Mt. Tabor. During one of my Masses in Europe, a man who had been out of the Church since he was a boy claimed he saw Christ "all in glory but with His wounds, and with His lips moving as though speaking to someone," standing in my place at the altar. In the sacristy after Mass he excitedly told me this vision lasted from the Consecration to my Communion. A fervent confession and complete amendment of life convinced me that he had seen with his bodily eyes what we priests should see daily with the eyes of faith.

If St. Francis of Assisi had been a priest, imagine how he would have offered Mass after the miracle of Mt. Alverno! Yet it depends upon you to have the stigmata in your heart in order to celebrate as fervently as would the Seraphim of Assisi.

Ask our Lady to give you the graces of graces: that of a daily increase in a spirit of lively faith, and of a daily advance in love as you offer the Holy Sacrifice. Even though it be for only one half-hour, try to have some of the fervor of the Curé of Ars. Afterwards you certainly will have the apostolic and missionary powers of St. Francis Xavier, even though you do not have his gift of miracles.

Note well, however, that I am not speaking of sensible devotion, nor feeling. Not at all. I am speaking of the fervor that is based on a lively faith, that is fed by meditating on this great mystery, and that is increased by having great desires.

Unfortunately, we become too accustomed to the sublimity of our Mass. I dare say with feelings of adoration and gratitude that it is partly the fault of our Lord Himself, for He has given us too much. It is in this above all that He has loved us, His friends, to excess. If Mass were a rare privilege, for instance, an extraordinary recompense for a high degree of generosity we have shown in our ministry or for some miraculous conversions brought about through our heroic sacrifices, it would be different. But no, Mass is an every-day affair, for the saintly as well as for those large numbers of priests who never think of becoming saints, but who have, at the same time no intentions of giving up such a great privilege.

"If you knew the gift of God. . ." (John 4:10). If you were enlightened by a more assiduous spirit of prayer, and by a more ardent faith; if above all your life were deeper and more intense, how you would appreciate the gift of gifts of your priesthood, the most sublime function of your ministry, which daily makes of you at the altar a true Christ! I am convinced that even the greatest saints have had overwhelming surprises in heaven when they understood in the light of glory what it means to celebrate the Holy Sacrifice of the Mass.

I remember witnessing at Naples the miracle of St. Januarius. After having had the privilege of holding in my hands the vial containing the congealed blood that was shed a thousand years ago, a few minutes later, before my very eyes, I saw this same blood ruddy, seething as it was the day the saint was martyred. I was affected but only momentarily. A minute later I remembered my chalice, the mystery of the transubstantiation of my Mass, and I lost my emotion. There is no doubt about it, I had seen a great miracle. But the miracle of my Mass is even greater. In fact between the two there is an infinite distance.

I am waiting for my last hour lovingly to challenge my guardian angel. I am going to tell him: "Through the mercy of Jesus, soon I hope to be your companion for all eternity. But despite my great misery, I will forever be more beautiful than you, for I will bear in my soul a likeness you do not have, a likeness to the Lamb of God stamped upon me by the Blood of the Lamb.

"And still more: for all eternity I will be more noble than you — not by nature but through mercy — for the Lord is of my race and of my blood, and through condescendence His Father is my Father and His mother, my mother. And so He is my eldest Brother, a title you do not possess.

"Dearly beloved Angel, listen to this, the height of glory: even as I adore with you the All-High, in truth I can glory in having commanded my God at the altar where He always obeyed me. Thus in virtue of my priesthood, I have been the master of my King and Master, a power and privilege you never had."

My guardian angel will answer: "So be it, sing forever the greatness and the mercy of the Lord, who has raised you above the Princes and the Thrones of Heaven."

Even if our Lord, to test my faith, offered to take me up each morning to the third heaven like St. Paul, or to allow me here below to enjoy the treasures of paradise, and all this in exchange for my Mass, I would fall on my knees and beg Him to allow me to keep until death my sacred right to stand at the altar. For this privilege I would freely renounce the charisms of St. Paul and all the saints. For they are pale rays from the sun of glory and of love, the Holy Sacrifice of the Mass!

* * * * *

It is not enough to be convinced of the beauty and the grandeur of your Mass. You must *want* to live it and know *how* to live it. This means that once you leave the altar you should as far as possible live as did the Blessed Virgin after the Annunciation, for like her you bear within you the God-Emmanuel.

Listen to what St. John Eudes has to say on this subject:

"The Holy Sacrifice of the Mass is so sublime that we would need three eternities to honor it worthily. The first would be by way of preparation; the second to celebrate the divine mysteries in an ecstasy of love; the third would be to bless and thank the Lord for this incomparable gift.

"Yet we will have only the third eternity to return adequate thanks, and for many of us this eternity will be spent making reparation for our tepidity and our shortcomings at the altar."

Earnestly ask our Lady for the grace of knowing how to make your daily Mass the heart and center of your interior life and of your active ministry. Your entire life should gravitate around the Holy Sacrifice, which through your deep faith and love will then become more than ever a well-spring of divine life for those around you and for many others near and far. This means: *Live your Mass, live for your Mass, live from your Mass.*

To help you do this, here is a practical suggestion: make your favorite prayer and practice the saying of the Offertory prayers, the formula of the consecration of the bread and wine, and the prayers immediately before Communion beginning with *"This is the Lamb of God. . ."* I call this practice the "Mass of St. John," because it is a short form of the Mass containing its true essential elements. Learn these prayers by heart or carry a leaflet in your Breviary. Say them in spare moments or when visiting the Blessed Sacrament. This priestly practice will help you to live your Mass.

Prepare and celebrate your Mass each morning as though it were the first and last Mass of your life. If you have truly mastered this science, you know everything: "and all these things shall be given you besides" (Matt. 6:33).

* * * * *

One final word concerning the efficacy of your Mass in relation to the conversion of souls. I repeat: any priest who tries to be a true Christ at the altar is by that very fact a true apostle. How few are those whom the priest reaches through his preaching and his ministry! But through his Mass he can influence souls all over the world. The reason is obvious: It is Jesus Christ Himself who, renewing His redemptive sacrifice through our hands, offers to His Father this triumphant prayer: "Father forgive them . . . hallowed be Thy name . . . Thy kingdom come . . . Thy will be done. . . ."

In this regard let me quote another striking thought from the late Bishop Tissier of France:

"Sometimes I hear discouraged priests complaining of the sterility of their ministry and that the only thing they can do is to celebrate Mass in an empty church.

"The only thing they can do? But they are saving sinners, they are the ransom for the guilty nations and they are bringing salvation to a world which certainly would burst asunder were it not for those redemptive Masses."

How explain those otherwise unexplainable conversions except by the Holy Sacrifice of the Mass? How account for the veritable Pentecost of grace we sometimes receive all out of proportion to the efforts and time we spend in our active apostolate, except through our Mass? Believe me, it is your chalice which cries to heaven for mercy, for it overflows with the Precious Blood: "Behold the Lamb of God, behold Him who takes away the sins of the world."

How much more effective and fruitful would be the marvelous apostolate of your Mass, if you added to the *ex opere operato* of the sacrifice itself the faith of St. Francis Xavier, the fervor of the Curé of Ars or of St. Vincent de Paul. Be sure of one thing: before God your mission has both its starting point and its crowning grace in your daily Mass. Offer your Mass with such fervor that the sublime prayer of Jesus at the Last Supper will be realized at the altar: "Holy Father, . . . that they may be one even as we are one" (John 17:11).

Make your mass an anticipated heaven and the perfect ransom for the souls entrusted to your care. And make the Mediator and the Victim of your Mass the "Deus meus et omnia" of your entire life. This is the way to become each morning at the altar the "disciple whom Jesus loved." (John 13:23). But at the same time, by your intense love, your faith, and your fervor, as you go to the altar, be also the "disciple who loved Jesus."

* * * * *

Whatever you give to Mass in the way of purity, spirit of faith, fervent prayer, is certainly benefiting your own soul as well as the souls of others. What a powerful means of sanctification and salvation is the chalice!

Never forget that the Holy Sacrifice of the Mass must be your greatest sermon as well as the most perfect priestly homage you can give to God. Make every effort to be a Christ at the altar, especially by careful preparation for Mass. Your Mass will be what your preparation has been. What your Mass is, that you are in the eyes of God. *Qualis Missa, talis sacerdos et talis apostulus.* One day you will be judged according to the amount of purity of faith and love you have put into the offering of the Holy Sacrifice.

Avoid one thing at all costs, and that is saying Mass out of routine.

At the Memento for the dead pray especially for the souls of deceased confreres. If you help them today, one day you will be helped a hundred times over.

May you hear these words of the Father every morning when celebrating Mass: "This is my beloved Son in whom I am well pleased. . . ." and those other words of Jesus, "This day you will be with me in paradise . . . . and on Calvary."

Yes, it is really paradise and Calvary, the altar of our daily Mass!

He has regarded the humility
of his handmaid. Because I was
little I pleased the Most High
(Luke 1:48; Liturgy).

4. Mary and Humility

This entire conference will be offered as a filial homage to the Immaculate Heart of Mary, mother and Queen of Apostles. In her school we will meditate on three great priestly virtues, beginning with the one that is at the base of all holiness: *humility*.

For every height there is a corresponding depth. In the divine plan, Mary occupies the highest place among creatures. Mary is the highest summit of the earth, touching God, bordering, as it were, on the Blessed Trinity.

By means of her unique, incomparable eminence, we can measure the depth of the abyss of the humility of Mary. She is the greatest, the holiest of creatures, because she was the smallest, the most humble.

* * * * *

The Gospels confirm and elevate certain virtues known to the pagan world, such as the Chinese family traditions of filial respect and obedience. In this case Christianity merely had to build on the solid ground of natural goodness.

On the other hand, Christ revealed to us the beauty of, and has imposed on us the practice of, certain virtues completely unknown before His time; for instance, the forgiveness of injuries, the love of one's enemies, virginity and chastity, but above all, it is safe to say, the eminently Christian virtue, humility of spirit and of heart. And perhaps, I might add, the one most difficult to practice. Why? Because it is diametrically opposed to the most firmly rooted tendency of our fallen nature, disordinate self-love.

The Word became flesh and capable of dying in order to prove to us His infinite love; "For God so loved the world . . ." (John 3:16). But it seems quite evident to me that He also chose the path of suffering to give us a serious and much-needed lesson, saying to us, as it were, "If you really want to belong to Me and come after Me, choose this infallible path: follow Me by humbling yourself, and you will find Me."

This is so true that the touchstone of true Christianity is and always will be the virtue of humility. Strictly speaking, it is possible to be chaste in heart and in body, and yet be a demon in pride. Remember the frightening case of the convent of nuns at Port-Royal near Paris, whose superior was the renowned Mother Angelique. Infected with Jansenism, they proudly refused to submit when Rome condemned the heresy. Archbishop Perefixe of Paris said of them. "These Sisters are as pure as angels, but as proud as devils." More fundamental than purity, important and delicate though this be, is the virtue of humility.

* * * * *

Humility consists on the one hand of a feeling of deep reverence before the majesty of God, and on the other hand, of a sincere and frank acknowledgement of our great weakness. But it is not sufficient merely to acknowledge our misery, for at the sight of it we could be provoked and even angry. Such is the case of a girl angrily breaking the mirror that reveals a physical defect.

Hand-in-hand with the recognition of our weakness must go peace, and even more, *love of our weakness*. When St. Teresa asked our Lord why He so loved humility, He replied, "Because I love the truth."

Therefore, humility and truth are convertible terms. I love my weakness, my spiritual poverty, my helplessness, because I love the truth more than I love myself. Without this peace and love, humility is impossible.

This is an attitude that was never found among pagans. The non-Christian might acknowledge his weakness because it humbled and shamed him. But this is precisely the reason that this virtue is so rarely found even among the good. As a matter of fact, it is easier to find a mortified man than one whose humility is as great as his austerity. An example of the latter would be the quite recent and wonderful case of Charles de Foucauld, the humble penitent and apostle of the Sahara desert.

Because humility is such an extraordinarily difficult and delicate virtue, however, it is the outstanding characteristic of great souls. A Russian Orthodox diplomat said of St. Pius X, as he stood before his coffin, "He was more the pope, more the representative of Christ, because of his humility than because of the tiara!" If you want your people to praise you sincerely, live so that they may say the same of you.

Yes, let them praise you for your zeal; let them admire you for your charity toward the poor and the sick, but let them also be able to say of you what a skeptical curiosity-seeker said of the Curé of Ars: "They talk a great deal of the miracles of the Curé of Ars. Well, as far as I'm concerned, the greatest miracle of all is his humility."

* * * * *

Let us now consider the three foundations of our humility. The first, and most evident, is our natural helplessness in the physical order. For instance, a man in the pink of health can be laid low by the bite of an insect, a draft of air, or an invisible microbe. And yet we are proud of ourselves!

Here is an interesting case: A monk had consecrated the best years of his life to the study of manuscripts, and as a result, his health broke. Nevertheless, he had reached his goal; he had found what he was looking for

49

and the results of his long years of research were contained in carefully written notes. He had a magnificent file, a monument of erudition . . . now people would take notice of him!

But what happened? One night a spark set fire to his manuscripts and in a few minutes the fruits of his years of unwearying toil were a pile of ashes. So upset was the poor monk that he went out of his mind.

This reveals what we really are: tiny ants, upset by a mere trifle. And when we find ourselves face to face with the unleashed powers of nature — a hurricane, a storm at sea, an earthquake or an erupting volcano — our helplessness is even more evident. Yet we remain full of ourselves, proud of what we call our powerful minds.

All this is very striking. But it is nothing when we consider another embarrassing weakness: our power-lessness to do good. We have the explicit words of our Lord on this point: "Without me you can do nothing" (John 15:5). Note well that He uses the word *nothing*. He did not say, "You can do something," but "NOTHING, without me." Not even an ejaculation can be said with merit without Him — nothing!

Yet there is something worse than this. Worse than nothing? Yes, indeed! For there is in each one of us a frightening tendency toward evil. Have no illusions on this score: *any one of us is capable of committing the worst of crimes!*

"Lord," said St. Philip Neri, "place both of Your hands on my head, for if You withdrew one of them I could betray you this very night, even worse than Judas did." And he was telling the truth, for we carry within us, as it were, a nest of vipers, lying in wait for a moment of inadvertence on our part, a moment of weakness, to do their deadly work. This explains the fall of the "cedars of Lebanon," the stars of Heaven. As I write this I have to remind myself, if I am not humble and prudent, tomorrow I could be what St. Paul called a "castaway." And note well that when a giant cedar falls in punishment for pride (I am speaking now of the fall of a consecrated soul, a priest, for example), the fall from such a height is a frightening thing, *"corruptio optimi pessima!"*

Tell me, what do we have to be proud about? In reality we possess only two things: our good qualities and talents — a treasure that belongs to God alone and is merely loaned to us — and our terrible misery, concealed in every one of us and belonging exclusively to us. Can we possibly be proud of our misery without being considered a fool?

That you may never be guilty of this culpable foolishness, have a strong hatred — stronger than you have for impurity — for the most impure of all impure loves, that of self-love and pride! Fear it as the capital vice of all vices. Friends of our Lord, who one day became traitors, fell for the most part because of pride, the root of a thousand other dreadful weaknesses. Remember the case of de Lamennais of Tyrrell and Loisy?

If you knew with what severity our Lord often punishes here below the revolt of the proud! I have seen the case of Nebuchadnezzar in the person of a rector of a university, horribly humiliated because of his terrible pride and his blasphemies. He was struck down, not by a mental affliction, but by a strange disease, which without causing the loss of his use of reason, forced him to live for two years like an animal, degraded in a way that cannot be described. Be on your guard; have a healthy and holy fear of succumbing one day to this disease of pride, cause of all scandals and of all failures.

* * * * *

What is the best way to defend oneself against this enemy? The answer is simple and practical. There are two ways to attack at its very roots and to become, little by little, humble in spirit and of heart.

The first means to use is one I do not hesitate to call infallible: that of *obedience to one's bishop or superiors* — but *perfect* obedience. Obey, bend your character to the yoke of submission without reservations, love to be directed, prefer the opinions and likes of your superiors to your own, follow their directives, and you will have a granite base on which to build the edifice of your priestly life.

Never forget that your success in the eyes of God (and this is the only success that matters) is closely tied in with your spirit of obedience. Yes, God will always give you graces in abundance if you come to Him by the path of obedience. When you make a mistake, the virtue of obedience will correct the error and double your merit. Leave the responsibility to those in authority, and remain in the peace that comes to those who obey. In a certain sense they enjoy a sort of moral infallibility: they will always be right, even when, objectively, they are wrong, for obedience is the surest guarantee of being right before God.

Learn to act in this supernatural way. Acquire these divine convictions. Make use of this criterion, so different from the wisdom of this world. This is the way the saints reasoned and acted. Basically this is nothing else than the "foolishness of the cross" of which St. Paul speaks, but which should be the one and only wisdom for you. We are living in a difficult period, one that is quite opposed to this doctrine. We breathe in everywhere the stifling, deadly, poisonous gas of revolt. That is why it is of the utmost importance for us to lean heavily on this eminently evangelical and supernatural principle of obedience.

Be on your guard against a certain spirit of arrogance and disordinate independence which is raging all around us. In this regard we are passing through a terrible crisis. But the Church will always be the guardian of fundamental principles. However, it is up to us priests to be living examples of these principles and not merely to speculate on them and preach them to others.

What a sublime example the Master has given us on this point! At Nazareth He was "subject to them" (Luke 2:51)! During His Passion, He was "obedient unto death" (Phil. 2:8). Imitate this incomparable model. Put your whole heart resolutely into this task, for it will pay rich dividends in the future.

Now for another practical piece of advice. What is the second means of blocking the flood of pride and of learning the lesson of humility? I reply by asking you a question. What is the best way to learn a language? By practicing it and sometimes even by murdering it, so as to speak it fluently. When I was in Korea, missionaries told me the story of one of their number who had a hard time mastering the language. Once when preaching to men on heaven, he used the wrong inflection and, instead of saying, as he intended, "Heaven will one day be your reward," he solemnly told them, "One day your reward will be a lady's hat!" This is learning the hard way.

In your dealings with those in authority and among yourselves, you have plenty of occasions. You will find them in your daily life, if you cooperate with grace. Remain silent when you are blamed for something which could easily be explained. "But Jesus kept silence" (Matt. 26:63). Swallow that bitter pill. And if a confrere, for example, has hurt you in a moment of excitement or through carelessness, go and shake hands with him, do something for him in a friendly way, to master your nerves and to place a restraint on your heart, vibrating with feelings of indignation and desires to assert its rights.

Through this practice do violence to yourself, and you will acquire that meekness and humility of heart so indispensable to your priestly ministry. We know the beautiful theories by heart. It is even possible to write magnificent dissertations on the grandeur of humility and at the same time be burning up with pride. Learn this divine language by *practicing* it daily.

The third and final basis for humility is our helplessness in our ministry. I refer to our absolute powerlessness to touch and convert souls, despite our eloquence, our knowledge, and our hard work. Once more, without Him who "gives the increase," we can do nothing. Even though you have labored throughout the night, casting your nets right and left like the apostles, Jesus has kept to Himself the secret of catching souls, and He reveals this secret only to those humble souls who He knows will not attempt to rob Him of His glory.

How mortifying it is after so much tiring labor, to have nothing but empty hands, when in our vanity we promised ourselves a tremendous harvest! Have no doubt about it, you can do a great deal of good, but only on the condition that you possess a great store of humility.

After many exorcisms, a priest commanded the evil spirit to leave the possessed person. Much to his embarrasment, the devil answered, in a tone of irony and triumph, "I refuse to leave." "And why?" demanded the priest. "Because," answered the devil banteringly, "You and I are cousins, we are both proud!"

This answer explains the sterility of our ministry. The devil resists our efforts in the pulpit, in the confessional, and in our ministry, because we are lacking in humility. The proud priest has no power over the angel who fell through pride.

On the other hand, we see how divine Providence always uses little people, "nothings," to accomplish great things in the Church. Often when God wants to renew Pentecost, to stir up souls by an extraordinary and miraculous event, His instrument in general is a straw, a child. Isn't this the case of St. Margaret Mary at Paray-le-Monial? of Bernadette at Lourdes? of Thérèse at Lisieux? With these grains of sand, our Lord overturns the world. With straws from Bethlehem, he sets fire to the stars. Fortunate then, a thousand times fortunate are the humble, the little ones. "The weak things of the world has God chosen to put to shame the strong!" (I Cor. 1:28).

Do you really want to become the intimate friend of your King and Savior? Do you truly want to glorify Him in the work to which He has certainly called you? Do you sincerely wish to become docile instruments to carry out His plans? Then be humble, very humble, and you will win His Heart. Then in this Heart you will find the secret of saving, of converting, of sanctifying souls, His treasures and your heritage. Say often with your lips, but more often with your deeds, this beautiful prayer: "Jesus, meek and humble of heart, make my heart like unto Thine!"

Every morning during your thanksgiving, promise the Heart of Jesus to accept generously the *humiliations of the coming day*. Offer them to Him in exchange for certain conversions you have in mind, whose greatest obstacle is often too much reasoning, a great lack of humility. Unbend yourself, humble yourself, that they in turn may unbend, docile to the action of grace. Acquire humility by humbling yourself and by perfect obedience of spirit and heart!

*At the cross her station keeping, stood
the mournful mother weeping.*

5. Mary and Sacrifice

When the Word of God decreed that He would save us through the shameful death on the cross, one thing was lacking for the carrying out of this divine plan: the capacity to die. Because of His divine nature He was immortal life itself.

Then it was that He had recourse to Mary, asking of her not only His human nature, but also her free cooperation in the work of salvation, which was to begin with the Incarnation and to end on Calvary. Mary's *Fiat* was decisive in the mystery of the Redemption. Thirty-three years later, at the side of the crucified God, she obtained the marvelous title of Co-redemptrix.

It is quite evident, then, that the Savior willed to associate Mary with every phase of His work. This is so true that, even though He could have saved His mother from every sort of bitterness, Jesus did not spare her one tear. In fact, on Good Friday, He crowned her Queen of Martyrs and Sorrowful Mother.

"Well-beloved Mother of Apostles, Queen of the Cenacle, appointed to continue the work of your crucified Jesus, which is also your own, by the martyrdom of your sorrowful Heart, teach us the great lesson of Calvary, and help us generously to practice it for the glory of your Son and for the glory of you, His Mother!"

* * * * *

Priests — truly apostolic priests — are no strangers to the subject of sacrifice. In fact, self-denial — sometimes to the point of heroism — is the daily bread of the priest. Nevertheless, permit me, unworthy though I am, to speak about the spirit of immolation, the very essence of your priestly calling.

If, like St. Paul, you had to draw up a list of your daily crosses, it would certainly be a long one. Briefly, let me sum them up for you. They fall under two headings: physical crosses, and the ones we call moral or spiritual.

Physical crosses are usually of a personal kind, and are often aggravated by the very nature of the active life we lead as priests and missionaries, active beyond the limits set by human prudence. Take, for example, the cross of bodily infirmity. You have no time to pamper or even take proper care of your body, occupied as you are with priestly duties. Especially in the missions, how easily it succumbs to the attacks of various diseases, worn out as it often is by incessant travelling and intemperate climate.

Then, because He knows it is good for you, our Lord completes your immolation, impressing on your body the likeness of His own wounds, allowing you to share in His sufferings. Generous priests are not afraid of what St. Francis called "Sister Sickness." Not only does it not frighten them, it does not even stop them. They bank on this priceless treasure to help them pay the ransom for their flock, to purchase their conversion. At this time they say with St. Paul: "For when I am weak, then I am strong" (II Cor. 12:10).

A greater source of suffering for many a priest is the isolated life he is forced to lead. Even the fact that he has God of the tabernacle as his faithful companion and friend does not make him indifferent to his loneliness, and consequently does not take away the merit of this particular kind of suffering — for some, great suffering. There is no question about it, this type of cross is, in general, a hard one to bear, for, with the exception of a special vocation, it is difficult for a priest to accustom himself to living separated from his confreres, often with the feeling that he is forgotten and abandoned. This was one of Father Damien's greatest sacrifices.

But I do not hesitate to say that if this first category of crosses were the only one the generous priest was called upon to bear, he would seriously begin to wonder if the good Lord had lost confidence in him or was unwilling to accept his total offering. Happily, this is not the case, for physical crosses are but the first step in his ascent to Calvary. *Moral and spiritual crosses* are to be found in the life of every priest — keen sufferings that sometimes border on martyrdom. There are a few which we have all experienced and which, like St. Lawrence, we can point to as our greatest treasure.

First of all, there is the terrible, incessant warfare unleashed by the devil to counteract the effects of your ministry. How often we priests are overwhelmed at the thought of the dangers which we foresee for the souls of our people, whom we love so much! Then it is that a priest is tempted to say with Moses: "Either save them, Lord, or efface me from the book of life" (cf. Exod. 32:32). Missionaries exiled by the Communists from their people know what this suffering is.

Sometimes our Lord permits a relative victory for the enemy, allowing you to taste the bitterness of defeat. Your voice is like that of one crying in the wilderness; the seed you sow falls on rocky soil or among the thorns; your nets break because of the fury of the waves: not for you is the satisfaction of a miraculous draught! How heartbreaking it is for a priest, wearied in soul and body after so much hard work, to realize the futility of his devoted efforts. He wears himself out without always seeing the results of his self-sacrificing labors: "What profit is there in my blood?" (Ps. 29:10).

And as though this chalice were not bitter enough, suddenly all sorts of difficulties arise, adding to the contradictions and troubles already experienced. Instead of help and encouragement he waited for, the priest sees nothing ahead but a dark and gloomy horizon. If it were not for his Mass and the presence of our Lord in the tabernacle, the priest would often be tempted to ask to be transferred to a more fruitful field. This is particularly true when a wave of discouragement sweeps over him as he drinks the chalice of ingratitude of certain souls, for whom he has done so much, and who repay him with cowardice or forgetfulness when he really needs their help.

How many times the priest is convinced he knows by personal experience the meaning of the *taedium*, the terrifying anguish of the Heart of Jesus at Gethsemane! Then his own bitterness seems to parallel to some degree the cruel and poignant suffering of the Savior in His agony.

Add to this list the destruction caused by some natural catastrophe. After long years of hard work, of begging for funds, of worry and sleepless nights, disaster suddenly strikes and in a few hours or even minutes, the fruits of years of toil are swept away. Then it is you are tempted to ask, "Why? Dear Lord, why did You permit?" But, knowing well all this was permitted by a wise and loving God, you say "Fiat," and start all over from scratch.

Isn't it true, with some variations, that this is the actual experience of each and every one of us? This is what we call the martyrdom of everyday life.

Let us now turn the page to the great, divine lesson taught by these crosses and trials. What do the wisdom of God and the love of Jesus have in view when causing you to live and work under such pressure? The answer is: Their glory in you, and Their glory through you!

Their glory in you means above all and before all your *personal sanctification*. This is an inexorable law: If you are obliged to be saintly priests in order to become successful apostles, the cross is indispensable. You preach the cross in order to save and to Christianize the souls of your brothers; but it is the cross which will make you worthy of such a lofty ministry.

You know better than I the history of the saints. And undoubtedly you have rubbed elbows with certain priests who have been models of unusual priestly virtue. Thus you know to what point suffering is the indispensable element to complete in you what is wanting in your prayer and in your Mass, in order to make of each one of you an *offerens et oblatio*.

Divine life is always preceded by death. In the degree

that this principle becomes a reality, you can say, "For to me to live is Christ" (Phil. 1:21). We have to die to live God's life and consequently we have to die to become saints. But your priestly life, made up as it is of such hard daily mortifications, is in itself a slow death.

How insignificant seem many of the added penances of the saints, excellent and admirable as they are, when compared with the inherent austerities of your daily ministry! Sometimes I wonder if certain penitents we rightly admire would have had the courage to live to the full and joyfully to practice another kind of austerity, that of your daily life, the most holy, the most divine, because it is the state of life willed by Almighty God for you.

There is no lack of crosses to make penitents and saints of you. Besides, it is not the cross itself that has the power to sanctify, but rather, love for the Crucified. Therefore you must love one and the other wholeheartedly, without separating the two: Jesus Christ and His cross, or better still, Jesus Christ in all your crosses.

It is this love of self-immolation which makes you desire and rejoice in the "baptism of blood," which should reproduce in you a divine resemblance to Jesus. He willed to become a victim that in His own blood He might mold His intimate friends and especially form holy priests, heirs of His chalice and of His Calvary.

In the future, when crosses come to you, no matter under what form, this is the time to say wholeheartedly with St. Andrew: "O blessed Cross . . . receive me from men and give me back to my Master, that He who redeemed me through thee, may receive me likewise through thee." Yes, the cross will bring to you the treasures of the Heart of Jesus, His graces of predilection, the secret of intimate friendship with Him, the great secret of priestly sanctity.

But there is something else. *Actually your self-sacrifice is the most supernatural of all your apostolic efforts.* How applicable to you are the words of the Savior: "and I, if I be lifted up from the earth, will draw all things to myself." (John 12:32).

Preaching is certainly a powerful means for conquer-

ing souls because our Lord so willed it: "Go and preach."
Add to this two-edged sword — the word of God —
the marvelous acts of our priestly ministry: the
administration of the Sacraments and its fruits, the only
treasure of which you are justly proud.

But there is still another source of blessings in your
work of saving souls and one which, in my opinion, has
not been sufficiently exploited: suffering and the very
weakness of the priest! In one sense, suffering is a more
efficacious form of preaching than words, no matter how
eloquent they may be. Pain is something that must be the
basis of all priestly acts, for it is a sap without which
neither apostolic works nor the prayer of the priest can
have the supernatural fertility which God expects of them.

Any priest who suffers, *and who knows how to utilize
his sufferings*, is by that fact alone a real apostle, even
though otherwise he is unable to perform his priestly
duties. According to the Savior's plan, suffering fills up
what is wanting in our apostolic activity. For all apostolic
undertakings are imperfect and incomplete in themselves
as long as our crosses are not there to crown our work with
success and make it truly fruitful.

Thus it is safe to say, that after Holy Mass, suffering is
the most perfect and most powerful means of apostolic
action. Furthermore, it is capable of radiating far beyond
the reach of your preaching and your works of zeal. No
doubt about it, your catechism classes, your schools, your
preaching, have great influence, yet always within a
relatively limited field. On the other hand, your crosses,
your trials — bitter setbacks, painful sickness — can have
repercussions that are well-nigh limitless.

* * * * *

Listen to this interesting example. A youthful
deacon was obliged to bear arms during the last war. As a
result of being struck by an exploding shell he was
grievously wounded; the doctors found more than thirty
wounds. Almost miraculously he survived, although a
physical wreck. But despite it all, he was obsessed with

this one thought: I must become a priest!

Finally, through friends, he obtained an audience with the Holy Father. Kneeling before the Sovereign Pontiff, he pleaded his cause: "Holy Father, grant me the great favor of allowing me to be ordained a priest so that I may save souls."

Greatly moved, the pope replied, "But how? You cannot preach, you are unable to work, you are an invalid."

"Most Holy Father," replied the sick man, "what you say is true; I could never be an active priest. But think how many souls I could save by uniting my sufferings to my chalice." And he continued to insist, "Holy Father do not refuse me the grace of being able to suffer and offer Holy Mass so that I may be an apostle."

The favor was granted, and I can assure you that with his Mass and his wounds, with his great sufferings and with great love, this human wreck is saving many souls. Already he may have reaped a greater harvest than many of us despite our active apostolate. And who knows? Perhaps some of you here have received, through the power of God, a shower of graces coming from afar, from the crosses and altar of this wounded veteran, wounded especially in his heart! Before God this invalid is a truly great missionary.

It seems to me that we have not sufficiently penetrated into this consoling mystery of the apostolate of our sufferings, as doctrinally true as that of Calvary. Never forget that, even though the preaching of Jesus was incomparable, He preached relatively little. On the other hand, His apostolate of suffering extended throughout His entire life from the Incarnation to Golgotha.

I mentioned that this is a consoling mystery. As a matter of fact, not all priests can continue preaching and working until they drop in their tracks. But everyone who, despite his years is privileged to remain on the battlefield, as well as those who are forced to relinquish their post and their arms to others, can and must — without exception — love while suffering and suffer with love, for the salvation of souls. In this way you can be an apostle until the moment of your death.

Once more I remind you of the lesson taught us on Calvary by Mary, Queen of Apostles and Queen of Martyrs. There is no question about it, all the preaching of the apostles never had the efficacy of those three hours of mortal agony at the foot of the cross. Mary was by no means merely giving us an example of her love for her Son. She was the incarnation of a profound doctrine. She was preaching what the Savior was preaching and practicing as He hung there nailed to the cross, namely, that there is only one way to save souls, and that is by mixing with the Precious Blood of the chalice our own blood, that is to say, our sufferings and our love. The more we are hosts — *offerens et oblatio* — for the salvation of souls, the more our priesthood will be exercised for the glory of God.

* * * * *

Always consider the sufferings and trials of your daily life — the ones that are a part of your priestly state — as your number one penance and as the great secret, after Holy Mass, of all apostolic success.

As a practical consequence, *love your crosses:* contradictions, criticisms, sickness; yes, love these providential penances, all the more so because you did not look for them.

Without this fundamental mortification, there can be no supernatural success, no divine harvest, for, "Without the shedding of blood there is no forgiveness" (Hebr. 9:22).

6. Mary and the Apostolate

Officially it was Peter who presided over the Cenacle. But Mary was there in her capacity as Queen of Apostles, and consequently as queen of Peter himself. Mary is the queen of the Cenacle because she is the mother of Christ the Savior. But more than this, she took part in and was the sole witness of some of the most sublime events of Christianity.

She is the sacred ark of the mysteries of the Incarnation, the infancy of Jesus, and His thirty years of hidden life at Nazareth. Who other than Mary could possibly have known of the miraculous generation of the Infant-God, and so of her virginal maternity?

It seems probable enough that Mary discreetly revealed these depths of grace and of redemption to the apostles, eager as they were after Pentecost to be instructed in these historical facts, whose key remained exclusively in her hands. I like to think we still preserve one of the most beautiful — and perhaps the most intimate — examples of these confidences in the daily recitation of the Angelus.

Let us then gather around the mother of the apostles, the gentle queen of the Cenacle. May our filial piety obtain from that Heart, which guarded the secrets and the words of the great King, the light and fire needed to help us carry out perfectly the mission that has been entrusted to us. ''Queen of Apostles, make each one of us a truly docile instrument for the accomplishment of the merciful designs of the Savior, your Son!''

"Come, follow me," the Savior has said to you. "Leave all things, for I will make you fishers of men . . . Go, preach the Gospel to all creatures . . . go and teach . . ." (cf. Matt. 4:19; 28:19).

This is your mandate, a divine mandate if ever there was one. In it is to be found the fundamental reason for your apostolic calling. You do not find yourself on this path of complete loyalty to Christ because of your own choice. "I have chosen you" (John 15:16), were His words to you. You are His messengers, and every one of you can say in all humility and truth with St. Paul, "I am an apostle of Jesus Christ," a title that is backed up by the God-given priestly character, and strengthened by all its powers.

* * * * *

Just what do we mean by the apostolate? Substantially it means: *with Mary and like Mary to give Jesus to souls; with Mary and like Mary to give souls to Jesus.* This definition seems to me to be both complete and substantial, for in reality you have no other end in view, no other obligation, than the complete realization of this ideal. Your goal is all the more glorious because it involves lifting souls out of the depths of paganism and this means the renewal of the apostolic marvels wrought by the first twelve messengers of the Good News. You are their legitimate successors; you walk in their footsteps, other Pauls and Francis Xaviers.

This being so, what is zeal? Zeal is "divine heat radiating from a divine fire." Here is another definition: Zeal is the anguish we feel at the sight of a God so little known and so much insulted; of so many souls in danger of perdition.

Both definitions presuppose the same foundation: a heart on fire, an all-consuming love, the heart of an apostle. For how can we warm others if we ourselves are not on fire? How can we feel anguish of heart at the sight of God so little known, if we do not love Him with a more than ordinary love? How love souls in danger of damnation and how devote ourselves to their salvation, if we are not burning with love for Him who first of all gave His life to save them and us? Thus zeal, true zeal, is nothing else but the logical and spontaneous expanding of a heart being consumed with divine love. Yes, he who loves, and only he who loves, can repeat the words of the apostle: For "The love of Christ impels us" (II Cor. 5:14).

Only those who have given their hearts entirely to the adorable Master can make their own and sincerely repeat the words He Himself addressed to St. Margaret Mary: "Being no longer able to restrain the flames that consume Me, I must spread them through you."

I think you have understood. When love consumes you interiorly you feel the need of obtaining relief by letting it overflow on others, by letting the fire within you enkindle the souls of those around you. Love and zeal, then, are actually the same thing. When we speak of an internal fire, we mean *love:* when we speak of flames radiating from a heart all on fire and feeling the need to spread fire far and wide, we are talking of *zeal*.

Listen to these words of St. Francis Xavier, which seem to spring from the depths of his heart: "Would, my God, that I could multiply myself and my work; would that I could give a thousand lives and die a thousand deaths to make You known by all creatures!" This is what we mean by zeal. Keep in mind that this doctrine of love turned into all-consuming zeal is all the more solid, inasmuch as the first commandment is always fulfilled and perfected by the second. A good example is that of Father Damien, whom I like to call a "martyr of the *First* Commandment — total love."

When we love God, and because we love Him, and solely in the measure that we truly love Him, do we love our neighbor, not only as ourselves, but more and to such a degree that we are ready to give up our time, our health, our rest and our very life. This is the case of every generous priest! He is the living confirmation of the definition of zeal given by William of Paris: "A flame from the furnace of the Holy Spirit."

* * * * *

And now what is the definition of a true apostle? *"A chalice filled to the brim with Jesus and overflowing on souls."*

Note well that I said, "filled to the brim with Jesus." This means that an apostle is not necessarily one who works a great deal, but with a mere spark in his heart. We could call such a one a good worker, but not a great apostle. All the apostles were wonderful workers, but, sad to say, not all hard workers are apostles.

An apostle, above all and before everything else, is one who radiates a divine fire, working when God wants him to, but likewise wearing himself out in the silence of the hidden life, without working, when this is God's will, and with astonishing success in the winning of souls. From among thousands of examples we cite that of the Star of Lisieux, St. Thérèse.

What was St. Francis Xavier? What was St. Thérèse of Lisieux? With two burning hearts, marvelous in their redemptive power, following two completely different paths, but equally great in their radiating, fruitful apostolic action, both were "overflowing chalices."

This is the reason I am so obsessed with the idea of preaching love for the Heart of Jesus to choice souls, especially to priests, as the foundation of all apostolic work. If the heart is not full of divine energy and blood is not beating strongly, how can we ask the hands to work, how can we hope to form apostles?

For too many, there is no fire, no motivation. Their love is weak. This is the reason why they bargain with God. This too explains their lack of success despite hard work, for again, it is not so much work that constitutes the essence of the apostolate, but rather the love that animates the worker.

How often we find priests by nature very active — perhaps too active — and who according to all appearances seem successful in their efforts. And yet it is easy to see that the lasting and genuine result of so much hard work is often lacking. Why? Because in all this activity there is more feverishness than love and true zeal. Only life can beget life, and only divine love is truly fertile. The best proof of this is the example of each one of the saints. There are no exceptions.

In the course of these conferences I will have occasion to remind you again of the necessity of a solid formation of the heart of the priest, of the need of teaching him how to love our Lord with a great love, in order to make of him, no matter what his field of work, a real apostle, a successful missionary.

But for the moment I beg of you, ask the Sacred Heart of Jesus and the Queen of Apostles for the gift which is the source of all fruitful apostolic activity, the very soul of your priestly ministry, the "knowledge of the love of Christ!" I am sure I am not wrong in saying that this is the secret of the success that has for long years accompanied the work of priests everywhere.

Blessed be the seminary which has formed priests "that you should go and bear fruit, and that your fruit should remain" (John 15:16).

* * * * *

Allow me now, respectfully but with conviction, to give you some advice concerning your apostolate. Never aim at what is called "success," behind which is often hidden refined self-love. Rather seek the glory of our Lord, as He understands it; work for the salvation of souls, but according to God's will. That is sufficient. "For my thoughts are not your thoughts; nor your ways my ways."

Success and the glory of God, success and the salvation of souls, are not always synonymous terms. There are even certain brilliant successes that are failures in disguise, just as there are setbacks which are blessings and hidden victories. And speaking of failures, do not fear them too much, for they do not always correspond to the reality which God alone knows.

Remember the failure of Calvary, humanly speaking the greatest in history. Yet see how it was all part of the plan of divine Providence, and how in reality it was the victory of victories: "O death, where is your victory?" (I Cor. 15:55).

Do your duty conscientiously and supernaturally, and allow our Lord as He knows best to draw His glory from your success, your setbacks, your failures: "For those who love God all things work together unto good" (Rom. 8:28).

And now I ask the Heart of Jesus to make you realize that it is truly He who is the inspiration of this doctrine. Let His Heart speak to you! When you are teaching catechism and preaching His Law, above all preach, I beg of you, "in season and out of season," the *adorable Legislator!* As the foundation of all your preaching, no matter what the subject, bring out forcefully the adorable person of our divine Lord, so little known, sad to say, by Christians, and even by those who call themselves His friends.

In your ministry, make a living reality of these words spoken by the angels to the shepherd on that blessed Christmas night: "For behold, I bring you good news of great joy which shall be to all the people; for today . . . a Savior has been born to you, who is Christ the Lord" (Luke 2:10-11).

Yes, before and after having explained the Law, be sure to stress the person of the Savior whose very name possesses unique power.

There is something seriously lacking in certain preachers and catechists who stress so strongly the positive law and the penal law but hardly touch upon the divine figure of Jesus Christ. It is quite possible to be a master jurist and to be familiar with the entire Napoleonic code without knowing the history of Napoleon. But you cannot be a true Christian, perfectly faithful to the divine Law, without knowing and intensely loving the Legislator, Jesus Christ. In the case of the Jews it was all right for Moses to remain in the background, provided they knew the Law. But as for you, bring out into the open the Sun who is the very soul of the Christian Law. "That they may know thee, the only true God, and him whom thou hast sent, Jesus Christ'' (John 17:3).

My long experience has taught me that everywhere there are numerous Catholics, especially among the graduates of Catholic schools, who know the entire Law by heart, but who are poor Catholics because they are both ignorant of and have no love for the divine Legislator.

* * * * *

Here is another important remark. As you preach the adorable person of Jesus Christ, be sure to insist with great conviction on His doctrine of charity; that is, preach His love, His Heart. ''I have come to cast fire upon the earth, and what will I but that it be kindled? . . . Come to me, all you . . .'' (Luke 12:49 and Matt. 11:28).

Never forget that, fundamentally, the great and divine novelty of the Gospel is that of a *God who loves* and who, to prove this love and to get us to love Him in return, did what St. Paul calls the ''foolishness of the cross'' which presupposes the ''folly'' of the Incarnation. Always remember that the First Commandment, *''diliges,''* is and always will be the first and the greatest, in every latitude and for every race, in Rome as well as in the Orient. The Second Commandment and all the others are founded on the first and flow from it.

Say and repeat in every language and in every dialect with a holy tenacity, that *God is love* and that His first right is to be loved *''ex toto corde et ex tota anima et ex tota mente,''* thus with our entire being.

With St. Paul, teach that ''he who loves his neighbor has fulfilled the Law,'' and likewise ''he who does not love abides in death'' (Rom. 13:8 and I John 3:14). If you build on this doctrinal rock neither the winds nor the floods of temptation or persecution will overthrow the house of the Lord.

Do not lay any other foundation, for this was the one laid as the cornerstone by all the apostles for the very first preaching of the Gospel. I am profoundly convinced that the theology which proved to be the opening wedge in a completely pagan world, and the Pentecost which brought about the astonishing expansion of Christianity in the first centuries of the Church, was the good news, the overwhelmingly good news from on high, that *God is love* and that He came to earth to beg our love at the price of His Blood!

I am sure you also have noticed, as I have, that this doctrine, which sums up the entire catechism, is the most catholic, the most universal of all our dogmas. For it is a dogma that everyone — children, youth and the aged, the simple and the learned — understand with astonishing clearness. It is the key, the only supernatural and adequate explanation of all the mysteries of our faith, without exception.

When your prospective converts ask you the "how" and the "why" of the facts of the Incarnation, the cross, the Eucharist, the Church and the sacraments, what other answer can you give save the one that shines forth like the sun from every page of the Gospels and in all St. Paul's epistles, "For God so loved the world that he gave his only begotten Son"; "He has first loved us"; "Jesus . . . loved them to the end" (John 3:16; I John 4:10; John 13:1)?

From this affirmation the conclusion follows logically: "Who would not love in return the One who has loved us so much? My child, give Me your heart."

If St. Thomas himself, like St. Paul, had been called upon to dispute before pagan intellectuals honestly and sincerely seeking to grasp the mystery of Christianity, he would not have found an answer more enlightening or more doctrinal. This must be the foundation of every Christian edifice, whether it be that of the Catholic University of Louvain, of Milan or of Washington, or that of the much simpler but no less important Christian edifices in mission lands.

"But we . . . preach a crucified Christ" (I Cor. 1:23). This is the Christ who is the way and the truth. But He, infinite Love, is also the revelation of His Father's love, He is our way, our redemption, our life; and tomorrow He will be our reward in heaven only because He is merciful Love.

Once more, base all your evangelical work on this, the most sublime, the most easy of access, and the most eternal of all truths: *"God is love."* Preach and teach that, in giving Himself to us through love, He asks only one thing in return: the gift of ourselves, our love. "Love therefore is the fulfillment of the Law" (Rom 13:10).

* * * * *

Each day before your Mass, ask the Mother of Fair Love to teach you the science of sciences, to obtain for you the gift of gifts, that of a truly all-consuming love for her Son, so that in her school you can become genuine apostles. Fervently ask that this love become a blazing fire, the motivating force and the divine obsession of your preaching and all your priestly work.

Any priest or missionary who is deeply in love with our Lord, and who, like St. John, knows how to pray, fight, and suffer in the Heart of His Master, will necessarily be a great harvester of souls, for the same love that makes a man a saint, likewise makes of him a true apostle.

For with thee is the fountain
of life (Ps. 35:10).

7. "Overflowing Chalices"

No doubt each one of you has a great love for the Blessed Virgin. Try to love her more and more, but be sure your love is proved by reproducing in your soul Mary's virtues so fitting for holy priests and genuine missionaries. From her motherly Heart we must learn the secret of divine success in our apostolate, for she is the queen and model of apostles. "All her glory . . . is from within," and I might add, "all her power is from within" (Cf. Ps. 44:14).

She exercised her silent but powerful apostolate from the 25th of March until Christmas; from Christmas until Calvary, and from Calvary until her glorious Assumption. From a Heart filled with God she was able to pour out God; because she was the most perfect reservoir containing substantial grace Himself, Jesus, her God and her Son, she was able to give Him to others. Besides, as universal mediatrix, she has at her disposal all the graces won by the Redeemer.

She never preached, but no one has ever been so much a missionary of the Father, and the apostle of the Son, *"from within."* This is one of the greatest lessons Mary can give to priests and to missionaries.

* * * * *

Despite the fact that evil is to be found everywhere, I

am still an optimist. Why? Because I believe in this divine statement, ''I am the resurrection and the life'' (John 11:25). But let me say at once that in recalling these words I am not referring principally to our Lord's presence in the Blessed Sacrament in our tabernacles. The tabernacle, despite its divine treasure, in itself is not enough. Look at all the evil surrounding our tabernacles, despite their number and despite the real Presence!

It is evident therefore, that the eucharistic tabernacle alone is not sufficient. According to the divine plan, to complete this tabernacle there must be next to it another one, the heart of a holy priest! Without this the eucharistic tabernacle can become the silent prison of the Lord Jesus. On the contrary, wherever a *saintly* priest ministers at the altar, the eucharistic tabernacle becomes an inexhaustible fountain of life. This is the explanation of the great success of priests like John Vianney, Vincent de Paul, Francis Xavier, and Don Bosco.

Let us put it another way. If He had so willed, God could have surpassed the bridge and the canal we call Mary, something He has not done nor ever will do. God expressly willed that Mary should be the indispensable mediatrix of the Incarnation, and thereafter the mediatrix of all graces, even though He could have distributed them Himself. What is true of Mary is also true of the priest.

The priest is, by the will of God, a necessary mediator with Christ the Mediator. We also have been appointed as dispensers of grace, as a bridge between the crucified Mediator and souls. But we exercise this mediation not only by working for souls and distributing the Church's treasures, but also by becoming, like Mary — a mediatrix, a radiating power, ''from within.'' The great secret of priestly success is to be found in a priestly heart modeled on the Heart of the Co-redemptrix. As of Mary, so of the priest, ''all his glory, all his power, is from within.''

What then is supernatural fruitfulness? Divine life radiating from a heart made divine, whether in silence like that of Jesus in Nazareth or in full activity, as when Jesus preached to the multitudes.

And what is an apostle? *A chalice filled to the brim with God, with Jesus Christ, giving its overflow to souls,* like a St. Francis or a Little Flower.

Activity is merely the ordinary form of the apostolate, but in activity, excellent and necessary though it be, is not to be found its substance, its soul. The secret of every form of apostolate is to be found in a soul of great faith and in a heart on fire, in a profound interior life, in a breathing of the Holy Spirit "from within." Supernatural success is always far more the ripe fruit of this spirit of prayer than the result of our labors, our preaching, our organizations. These latter always presuppose the former.

A heart on fire, the heart of a saint — even though there be no external activity — of itself constitutes an apostolic power of the highest value. Again look at Mary and, following her example, the thousands of other silent "missionaries" preaching through love and suffering. Without this interior motivating power, intense activity is fever, not zeal; it is a voice crying in the wilderness. In fact, it can become a positive danger.

* * * * *

Here I would like to hand on to you two important lessons our Lord taught me during my long apostolic career.

The first of these lessons was a complete disillusionment for me, but at the same time a great grace. In the early days of my priesthood, I believed for a short time in the efficacy of learning, of eloquence, of apostolic works in themselves. This illusion did not last very long, for, without looking for them, I came across great masters in learning, in eloquence, and in activity, the three mirages which at that time fascinated me most. But our Lord wished to prove clearly to me that when these men were not masters and doctors of the interior life, of charity, of priestly holiness, they were nothing but the "tinkling cymbals," spoken of by St. Paul. Around them there was emptiness, a desert, nothing — and worse than nothing! Not only was there a frightening lack of fruit, but often ruins and corruption.

What would I not give to help you get rid of your illusions on this subject, and to replace them with quite another conviction: souls are saved above all by the holiness of the priest!

We all have our dreams, which often last a long time. Sometimes they turn into nightmares. Here is an example: a young priest came to me one day and told me, "Father, I need your advice. I am really discouraged. I am an assistant in a parish where the faith is at a low ebb, and am working with the pastor and other assistants, trying to help these people. For five years I've done everything possible to try to win them over, but the results are nil. I can assure you I've tried everything and it breaks my heart to have to admit there has been a complete failure."

Once again he repeated, "I've tried everything. Please give me some advice and encouragement, for I really want to be a good priest and to save souls. Please tell me, what *do* I have to do to save souls?"

Expressly I made him tell me again that he had tried *everything*, without results. Then I asked him, "Have you ever tried becoming a *saintly priest?*" And when, surprised, he answered "no," I told him, "Well then you haven't tried everything! You don't begin with the secondary things, like organizations, music, and processions, you begin with fundamentals, with the altar! On the altar is the tabernacle, and in it you know there is a ciborium, and in the ciborium a divine Victim. You must be that living victim, that sacred tabernacle, that ciborium — an *Alter Christus* — a saintly priest. First try this apostolate, and then one day, be it only in heaven, you will learn how God is faithful!"

Listen to what a priest who was a famous orator, writer, and servant told me after a conference I gave on this subject. Profoundly affected by what he had just heard, he said to a group of astonished young priests, "Yes, I can assure you that what Father has just told you is the truth, pure and simple. It is now more than thirty years since I began to write. I have to write well, for there is a market for my books, and through them I've made a fortune. Yet despite all this, I'm ashamed to admit that during these thirty years I've never known what it is to give absolution to one person affected by one of my conferences or converted by one of my books."

What a sad admission! And how many others there would be if priests were honest enough to reveal the truth about their ministry as it is seen by God and as known by themselves.

* * * * *

We come now to the second lesson which reads like a page from the Gospels. Wherever I have found what I call a "straw of Bethlehem" — a humble hidden soul on fire with love for our Lord — I have always found the explanation of great conversions, sometimes bordering on the miraculous. Let me give you a striking example which is better than a whole volume of brilliant dissertations.

Years ago I was brought to the room of a sick man who had been excommunicated because of his violent attacks against the Church. What a surprise for him to see a priest at his bedside!

"Get out of here!" he yelled at me angrily. "Get out of here at once!"

I answered, "I won't leave without having given you absolution in the name of the Sacred Heart of Jesus."

"Don't talk to me about Him," he cried even more loudly. "Get out of here fast, you don't know who you are talking to."

"I know, sir, you've been His enemy, and that you've wounded His Heart. But this Heart is open to receive you, and is ready to forgive you. He has sent me to beg you to accept His forgiveness.

"Never!" he burst out. "Get out of here!"

But I was determined to win him over through the power of divine mercy and so I began pleading with him:

"Sir, you hate Him and He loves you. Repeat after me, 'I love You Jesus, because You are Jesus.' "

Every time he came back with an answer filled with hatred, I would insist, "Say with me, 'I love You Jesus, because You are Jesus.' " Ten, twenty, fifty times I repeated this powerful phrase, and I was becoming convinced that despite himself it was hitting home, that he was deeply moved.

After perhaps a half hour, during which time he had stopped his tirades, I suddenly noticed tears in his eyes! Taking advantage of the opening made by grace I again urged him to repeat, "I love You Jesus because You are Jesus."

A moment of silence, of deep interior struggle and then he burst out sobbingly, "Oh yes, I love Him, because He loves me!"

Knowing that he had been conquered by the Heart of Jesus I put my arm around his shoulders. Then like Saul he said, "What do I have to do?"

"Make a good confession. I'll help you."

An hour or so later, his face radiating joy, he called his non-Catholic wife and their three unbaptized boys, told them what had just happened, and invited them to follow his example.

And now the epilogue of this story. In it you are going to find a striking confirmation of what I have been saying: wherever you find a "straw" — a little soul but a fervent soul — you find conversions, even miraculous ones.

Would you like to know who resurrected this "whole cemetery," as the pastor put it? A month later, with the archbishop's permission, I offered Mass in the room of this resurrected Lazarus. Surrounding him were the four newly baptized: his wife and their three sons. After Mass, they sang in thanksgiving the hymn "Christ Conquers." It was really beautiful, and true. Then came the ceremony of the Enthronement of the Sacred Heart as King of this newly won home.

Suddenly from the corner, where she had been kneeling and crying softly, the old cook came over to the sick man and said to him with great feeling, "Dear sir, at this happy moment would you allow me to embrace you?" Deeply moved, the convert held out his arms. Then the elderly domestic went on to say, "For more than twenty-five years I have been working for you and during that time you thought I was only a poor servant, your cook. Oh no! I'm going to reveal a secret to you. For more than twenty-five years I've been an apostle of the Sacred Heart of Jesus, offering up my prayers, my sufferings, my daily Communions and my Night Adoration, asking one great favor of the Sacred Heart; not to allow me to die, nor to see heaven, until I had first seen heaven in this home. Now it is done, I see it, the Heart of Jesus has conquered. Now I can die, my mission is finished."

Is not this sublime and overwhelming?

And do you dare to tell me that by your preaching and your Mass, that with the grace of your priesthood, you cannot work wonders like this? Certainly you can, but only on condition that you possess the same power of that hidden apostle — sanctity!

It will always be true that when the Kingdom of God is established within the heart of a priest, he will radiate holiness, for divine life always works of itself in the heart of a man of God. This is why St. Teresa of Avila made the striking statement, "A fervent monastery has walls made of crystal." She meant that the monastery would radiate life and the fire of charity far and wide by the very fact that its members were fervent. Even if this monastery is in an isolated spot, its cloistered silence makes it all the more eloquent.

How consoling is this solid doctrine! God in His wisdom cannot ask all to have the knowledge or eloquence of a St. Vincent Ferrer, nor the charisms of a St. Francis Xavier or of a Curé of Ars. But one thing He does expect of all of us is the faith and love of these saints, especially when celebrating Mass, when praying, and in our interior life.

Once more I say to all of you: Try out this powerful apostolate, the only one within range of young and old, of the healthy and the sick; the only one that is always fruitful, for this is the very soul of every successful apostolate.

We talk a great deal — too much perhaps — about the strength of the Left. For my part, I prefer to speak of "the weakness of the Right" — of God's friends. *The Left is strong because the Right is weak!* If only we priests, the extreme Right, were men of faith and love as were Francis Xavier and John Vianney!

How many times these words of our Lord to St. Margaret Mary have been abused because misunderstood: "I will reign through My Heart despite Satan and his agents." There are some who, basing their conviction on this statement, believe that as a reward for some kind of a badly understood devotion, the Heart of Jesus will crush our enemies and will reign in spite of them. But I dare say, "No! This is not what Jesus had in mind." Humbly but categorically, allow me to correct the false assumption in this interpretation. It is true, our Lord did state that He would reign despite Satan and his agents. But listen carefully: *He never promised that He would reign despite us, His friends and apostles.*

When we priests are not His true friends and apostles, when we are not fervent, when our life is one of mediocrity, when our ambition is to be just "good" priests, then we stop Him short on His road to victory. He will not reign if John, James, and Peter are not the saints they ought to be. Certainly He will reign despite Satan and his agents, either by converting them or crushing them, but only on condition that His friends are faithful; that close to the eucharistic tabernacle there is another tabernacle, the heart of a holy priest!

* * * * *

It is not beautiful churches or splendid organizations that are lacking. What is missing is what Father Chevrier used to call "spiritual basilicas." "Help me," he would say, "help me to build the only basilica truly capable of saving the world."

When someone, prompted by curiosity, would ask him

what he meant, he would reply, "At any cost I want to build a basilica whose foundations will be holy priests, whose pillars will be holy priests; a basilica whose sanctuary lamp will be a priest burning with love, whose pulpit will be the preaching of a holy priest, a basilica whose altar will be a holy priest saying Mass. This is the basilica we need everywhere, and the only one. What good are those marvels of art, bronze and marble, if they are staffed by ecclesiastical functionaries — good perhaps — but mere sacerdotal machines? Give me my spiritual basilica with a holy priest and I will resurrect a parish and an entire city!"

Yes, Father Chevrier was right. It seems to me we have not insisted enough on the "ex opere operantis" of the priest-apostle, of the missionary. There are too many priests who are falling back on the "ex opere operato" and who are satisfied with being honest administrators, irreproachable functionaries.

The standards of justice of honest men in the world are not sufficient for those who by vocation must implant life and who must implant it from the superabundance of their hearts. A good official may only be a good worker. But again I remind you that "worker" and "apostle" are not always synonymous terms. Christ selected you to be apostles, for he wants to make of you "fishers of men." Only the fervent priest and saintly missionary is truly an apostle and one whose work is blessed by heaven with an abundant harvest!

Take courage as you listen to these statements, for holiness is the only apostolate that depends upon yourself, and the only one that is always possible, whether at the age of thirty or eighty, in times of peace or trouble or persecution.

If a priest is truly a man of God, if he has a heart full of God, and if he offers his fatigue, his worries and his cares, his countless other sacrifices as a prayer and an oblation for souls, "Amen, amen, dico vobis," if this simple offering is united to the chalice of his Mass, it will work miracles which God may hide from him but which he will joyfully behold one day in heaven.

We have forgotten this. In the hustle and bustle of worries and work which have absorbed the attention of even the best of us, these truths have often been forgotten. But as I mentioned before, divine Providence is bringing us back to the fundamental truths with the help of striking miracles. The voice that preaches to us is simple, clear, eloquent. It is the voice of God. It comes from Lisieux, from Carmel.

Yes, Thérèse of the Child Jesus is a "vox Dei." Look at this insignificant child who became a veritable hurricane of graces and miracles which has swept through all parts of the world, but especially the missions, where she has showered down her choicest roses! This is her privilege and duty, for since 1927 she is, by decree of the Holy See, the patroness of the Missions as St. Francis Xavier is the patron.

And what does she tell us, this "vox Dei?" Exactly what Mary had already said at Nazareth and on Calvary, in fact what our Savior taught us in the silence and obscurity of Nazareth, where He was already as much our Savior as on the cross: that the apostolate is much more than eloquent preaching. *It is the divine life in the soul.* It is a soul filled with God, radiating.

If we need preaching — and we certainly do — we need a thousand times more to preach with our hearts, whether in the pulpit or out of it, for a saintly soul has the power to save the world through a life of immolation and prayer, even though he never utters a word.

This is the lesson of Mary at Nazareth. This is the wonderful and encouraging lesson of the Star of Lisieux: *You give God in the measure that you possess Him and love Him.* I repeat, St. Francis Xavier saved more souls by prayer and sacrifice than by his labors and his miracles. You will rarely find anyone who can speak and work as he did, but who among us cannot believe and love, and sanctify himself as did this saint?

You are priests ". . . that they may have life, and have it more abundantly" (John 10:10). But always remember that Jesus is athirst above all for the souls of His priests, His shepherds and missionaries. First He

82

wants to reign deeply in the hearts of each one of you, in order to sanctify you. Then and only then, and in the degree that He is Life of your life, will He reign around you and through you!

Let me sum up this chapter by citing parts of two inspired texts that, taken together, bring home its fundamental idea: "Be saints . . . that you may bear fruit and that your fruit may remain."

Holiness and fruitfulness are equivalent and synonymous terms.

* * * * *

Be very faithful in making a good monthly day of recollection. Promise not to miss it, if you can help it, for it will be a great source of grace for you.

Above all, resolve to make your annual retreat *in a real spirit of faith*. I stress these words, *in a real spirit of faith*. By this I mean, be truly recollected and keep the silence between the various exercises. We can never talk too much about the importance of a good retreat. To make a half-hearted, so-so retreat, means without doubt loss of the greatest grace of the year. .

Make it in silence and pray fervently. After a serious examination of conscience make a good confession with the best disposition possible. And make your retreat in common whenever you can, under a retreat master, for no one is a judge in his own case. From time to time we need the words of a stranger to wake us up and to remind us of our serious obligations. Take advantage of the extraordinary grace of a retreat and in silence and recollection listen to the voice of the Lord.

Try your best to say your Divine Office, "attente ac devote." Love your Breviary and it will no longer be a burden but a source of grace, of light and supernatural strength.

Heart of Jesus, burning with love for me,
inflame my heart with love for Thee!

I will be thy reward exceeding great.

8. Holiness, the Source of Happiness

When Jesus Christ restored all things by His cross and by His Blood the world was not changed suddenly into an earthly paradise. Divine peace, the peace which Christ alone can give, was left to His friends and followers as the source of true Christian happiness. Our Lord was so anxious to have us believe in the great value of this peace that He speaks of it again and again after His Resurrection: "Pax vobis . . . pacem do vobis. . . ."

Christ affirms the possibility of happiness even more clearly in the Beatitudes, enumerating at length those who, despite the thorns of life and the trials of exile, are to be considered "blessed" or happy here below. What Christian in the name of some so-called philosophy would dare to correct the Master's words on this subject?

The strong, clear statements of the Gospel are sufficient to make us believe that happiness can and ought to be the portion of those who bear the sweet yoke of Christ with great faith and love. But in addition to the words of the Gospel we have another argument in support of this thesis: the Gospel as it is lived in the lives of the saints, the happiest and the only truly happy people on earth.

The saints are happy — extremely happy — obviously with a relative happiness, but one that is very real and effective. From Our Lady singing her Magnificat down to St. Thérèse of Lisieux and Bernadette of Lourdes, all the saints can say with St. Paul: "In all my tribulations I am overflowing with happiness." All have served the Lord in joy and all have lived in unshakable peace in the midst of the storms of life.

Who worthy of the name of Christian would dare to doubt the supernatural happiness of the apostles as they came forth from the tribunal "rejoicing because they were judged worthy to suffer for the name of Jesus"? Like them and after them, there is the army of "one hundred and forty-four thousand sealed" of the Apocalypse, the innumerable legions of saints who lived in God and enjoyed God when on earth and whose happiness far surpassed that of all the Kings and Princes of this world despite their powers and pleasures.

It is interesting to remark, that in this deep supernatural happiness of the saints, in this peace which "surpasses all understanding," and which nothing and no one can take from them, the cross plays a most important part. Not only is it no obstacle, no negation of happiness, but according to the divine philosophy of the Gospel, according to the adorable Preacher of the Beatitudes, it is the fuel that feeds the flame of peace, a stimulant that every single one of the saints has sought after lovingly that it might intensify their own happiness.

According to worldlings, suffering and happiness, tears and peace, are mutually exclusive. According to Jesus Christ they complement each other. The saint loves and even seeks the cross, he embraces it and looks upon it as a treasure because with the Crucified it brings him a peace and joy with which no pleasure of earth is comparable.

To understand this doctrine well, think over these simple words of St. Thérèse of Lisieux: "For a long time, suffering has been my heaven here below and I can hardly imagine how I shall ever get used to living where joy reigns without any trace of sadness. Jesus will have to transform my soul, otherwise I shall not be able to bear the delights of eternity."

Judge by the following example whether happiness can be a reality in the midst of suffering, when someone lives up to the Gospel ideal.

One day after finishing a sermon I was asked to visit a dying workman who wanted to see me before he died. The room was poor and bare. Lying on the bed was a young man suffering from consumption, the signs of death already apparent.

"Are you Father Mateo?" he said, trying to raise himself up.

"Yes I am, and I am happy to come in answer to your request. What can I do for you?"

"Father, look at this picture of the Sacred Heart of Jesus, which you signed. It seems that you go about preaching that where this picture is received with faith and love, there Jesus enters as our King, and if we love Him greatly He stays in our home as a Friend who helps and consoles us. Father, I know this by experience. I have tried to love Him so much! And He has loved me. With Him I have always been so happy. I am only a poor working man. I have suffered and struggled but I have always been very happy with Him. I know I am going to die soon and I wanted to thank you and to tell you how true it is that one is always happy with the Heart of Jesus. But especially I wanted to see you so that you might sing a hymn of thanksgiving with me. I know the Magnificat. If you will begin it, my wife and children will join us in saying it."

I was so overcome that tears filled my eyes. The man seeing this said: "I see you are unable to speak; help me up and I will begin it."

Then, leaning against me for support, he made a great effort to sing on earth what he was going to sing in heaven: the peace and happiness he had found in the love and service of Jesus Christ. He died the next morning and reintoned his Magnificat in heaven.

Notice these words: "I have suffered and struggled. . . I am only a poor working man. . . .I have been so happy with Him."

To return to the beautiful thought of St. Thérèse which I just quoted, all the saints could have spoken as she did of the "folly of the cross," and with a like sincerity. All the saints were human as we are; all dreaded suffering; all, humanly speaking, trembled before the cross. But the love of Jesus and His all-powerful grace have transformed their lives and turned depths of suffering into well-springs of joy — a mystery that worldlings will never understand.

*****

Who better than the priest is in a position to live by and to realize in his own life this marvelous doctrine? Who, better than we, can and should be really happy in our vocation? Has not the priest, by the fact that he is a priest, withdrawn himself from the three things that are for many others sources of sin and unhappiness? He has voluntarily renounced purely natural pleasures, and the exaggerated searching after comforts, ambition and the pride of life, together with worldly interests and the seeking after money, all of which are opposed to the life of sacrifice of the priest. But these privations, however meritorious they may be, are only a negative element — important certainly, but not sufficient of themselves to make you happy. In fact, God wishes these earthly goods, legitimate for others, but which you have sacrificed for Him, to be adequately compensated for in your divine vocation.

Much more important in this question of priestly happiness is the positive element. Once you have broken the chains that bind you to this earth, our Lord gives you a twofold treasure which can be for you, as it has been for the saints, a source of the most pure happiness.

1. *"Christ loved us and gave Himself up for us"* (Eph. 5:2). . . . Jesus Christ delivers Himself entirely into our hands; He gives us His Heart. How often can it be said of some priests who have not sufficiently appreciated the grace of graces, the gift of gifts — their priesthood and all the benefits it brings them — those grave, kind words spoken by Jesus to the Samaritan woman: *"If you knew the gift of God"* (John 4:10). If you only knew what peace and joy could be yours in the exercise of your priesthood,

especially in offering daily Mass! Angels looking down upon priests who are unhappy and sometimes very unhappy must ask themselves what extraordinary thing a priest must do to be happy since he possesses the very source of happiness — well nigh infinite happiness — in his daily Mass.

Recall what has been said about the Holy Sacrifice of the Mass and you will have to admit that the angels are right in being astonished at those who say Mass daily and are not perfectly happy in spite of all the trials of life. If we could only understand this truth; Jesus is the priest's source of strength and joy; His Heart at the altar is the life of his life, to such a degree that all his difficulties, all his sorrows become sweet when mingled with the Precious Blood in the chalice. This truth is the underlying thought of St. Bernard's *Jesus dulcis memoria:*

> Jesus, the very thought of Thee
> With sweetness fills the breast!
>
> Yet sweeter far Thy face to see
> And in Thy presence rest. . . .
>
> To those who fall, how kind Thou art!
> How good to those who seek!
>
> But what to those who find? Ah! this
> Nor tongue nor pen can show —
> The love of Jesus, what it is,
> None but His loved ones know.
>
> Jesus! our only hope be Thou,
> As Thou our prize shalt be. . . .

This hymn has a solid theological foundation. Once a priest appreciates the priceless treasure of his vocation, of his daily Mass, then he will experience a foretaste of Heaven, especially when crosses complete what is lacking to his morning Mass.

Were not Mary and Joseph perfectly happy at

Nazareth in the possession of Jesus? Both lived by faith, but they knew how to appreciate the gift of God — the Child Jesus — and so in spite of their many and continual troubles they were perfectly happy. So it should be with the priest who has understood the sublimity of his vocation and of the treasure entrusted to him by God and the Church. Ask priests like St. Alphonsus Liguori, St. Philip Neri, St. Vincent de Paul, St. Francis Xavier, the Curé of Ars and Father Damien, and without exception they will tell you that the spiritual joys of the priesthood far surpass all earthly happiness.

2. If all that Holy Mass gives you — Jesus Himself and His Sacred Heart — does not satisfy you, there is still another source of happiness for the priest: the souls he has baptized and the very exercise of his priestly functions.

Les Buissonnets, the home of St. Thérèse, presents a beautiful picture. Louis Martin and his family formed but one heart and soul in enjoying the beauties of nature, the joys of family life and especially the joys of the supernatural life, because of their fervent piety. But still more beautiful is the picture of a priest in a parish or a mission, invested with spiritual paternity and surrounded by the members of his flock. After Holy Mass, nothing can compare with the power of the priest baptizing, making people Christians and children of God. Nothing can be more consoling than to train these souls, nourishing them with the bread of the Church's teachings and forming Jesus Christ in them. No earthly joy, no matter how noble it may be, is comparable to that of a priest giving Jesus, the Bread of Life, to a group of adult or child communicants for the first time.

What joy is greater than that of a priest in the confessional, who, by the power of his priesthood, breaks the chains of a sinner, restoring to him the rights acquired at baptism and the friendship of the merciful Savior?

Is not the joy you experience on a great feast — Christmas or Easter, the Feast of the Sacred Heart, or a feast of Our Lady — when you see your people coming to Communion in great numbers, not better than any earthly joy? There are times when the priest begins to enjoy the hundredfold promised to those who give up all for God and souls. No wonder a holy old priest once said, "What will Heaven be like, Jesus, if already here below I am experiencing so much of its joy?"

Even where others find nothing but sadness, the zealous priest finds reasons for rejoicing. When you are administering holy Viaticum to a dying person, all those around you are weeping. And even though you yourself may share their grief, still your heart sings with joy at the thought of Christ's triumph in this soul and of the Heaven which awaits him.

Then what about the miracles of mercy often wrought through your priestly ministry — remarkable conversions of which we are often the instruments, and which repay us in one short hour for long and painful sacrifices? Here is a personal example of the many you yourselves may have experienced:

I was saying good-by to a Bishop in whose diocese I had been preaching. A car was at the door to take me to the boat, for I was to sail that evening. Suddenly a man came running up to me and said excitedly, "Father, please come with me at once! My father is dying and refuses to go to confession."

I replied, "But there are a number of priests who will be glad to go with you — I have to catch a boat."

"Father," he answered, "I have already called three priests and he has sent them away. Please come with me at once! The dying cannot wait and the Sacred Heart will repay you."

Hearing this, the Bishop said, "He is right, Father, the dying cannot wait. Sacrifice everything and go."

Without further ado I knelt for the Bishop's blessing and got into the car. Arriving at the house, a spacious mansion, I entered the hall and met the wife and children, all excellent Catholics and crying bitterly. I said to them, "Do not cry as though you had no trust in God. Please kneel down and pray."

Then I asked them, "Do you really love the Sacred Heart? Do you believe in His love?" In the midst of their sobs they all answered, "Yes, we do."

"Will you promise to be more than ever a family of the Sacred Heart, a really fervent family, a eucharistic family?" Again they said they would.

"Will you promise to be apostles of the Sacred Heart, to make Him known and loved in exchange for the conversion of your father?"

"Yes, Father, we promise."

"Then, trusting in your promise, and in the name of the Heart of Jesus, I will go to the dying man while you stay here and pray."

Without knocking, I entered the sickroom and walked straight to the invalid who stared at me in astonishment. Immediately, I said to him, "I have come in the name of the Heart of Jesus to offer you His mercy. You will accept it, won't you, and go to confession?"

He answered, "Yes, I want to go to confession right away!"

After the confession was over, I called in the family. What a scene of joy as amid their tears they renewed their promise to be truly devoted to the Sacred Heart. As I left the house, I can assure you I felt as if I were going to die of joy.

It will always be true, "to serve God is to reign." That is to say, the faithful priest does not have to wait for eternity to be rewarded by the Heart of Jesus. Here below he begins to receive the "hundredfold" and with it the peace and joy which more than compensate for his daily martyrdom. And this is but a foretaste of what God has in store for you — things eye has not seen, nor ear heard, nor the mind of man conceived.

Meditate often on these consoling words spoken especially for the priest who tries to be loyal to his divine Master and his calling:

> "Behold, I am coming soon,
> bringing My recompense, to repay
> everyone for what he has done." (Rev. 22:12)

*As my Father has sent me, even so
I send you.* (John 20:21)

9. The True Missionary Spirit

The essence of holiness consists in divine love; consequently perfection is one and the same for all the saints. But if we consider holiness in the lives of individual saints — that is to say, according to their personal vocation and the circumstances of their lives — it is evident that all do not walk in the same path, nor do all have the same characteristics. What a marvelous variety there is among the saints in heaven and among those still struggling for sanctity here below!

God is admirable in His saints, for with infinite richness of shadings and variety, He reproduces in them His own beauty, which is ever ancient and ever new. This principle once established, it is evident that in the army of Christ's priests the highly privileged vocation of missionary has a spirit with clearly marked characteristics quite proper to this calling. Here then, among others, are five characteristics of the missionary vocation. And what is said of missionaries in the strict sense of the word is also applicable to all priests, for all are, in a certain sense, genuine missionaries.

SIMPLICITY

There must be a spirit of perfect simplicity; in a word, of evangelical holiness. There must be a great simplicity in your personal conversations with our Lord, that is to say, in your method or kind of prayer. We pray as we love. Prayer and love are two supernatural elements attainable by children as well as by learned priests.

Be very simple in your life and your rule of life: avoid all complications and formulas which will only embarrass you without being of the least advantage to your soul.

Be very, very simple in everything that concerns your spiritual life; it will be all the more solid and deep if it is exempt from "mathematical problems," as Cardinal Bourne so aptly said when speaking of the spirituality of St. Thérèse of Lisieux.

Do not overburden yourself with many devotions. Those which are obligatory are quite sufficient to sanctify you, and you cannot undertake the others in a life such as yours, so full of work and of unexpected demands on your time.

Simplicity, order and practical common sense usually go together, and this is what you need both for your own interior life and for the lessons of virtue and piety which you must give to others.

It seems to me that the common sense and simplicity of St. Vincent de Paul joined to the simplicity and learning of St. Francis de Sales, and the ardent apostolic soul of St. Francis Xavier, would make the ideal missionary. These three giants of sanctity are quite according to your spirit and your calling, and all three are a model for all by their incomparable simplicity and depth of learning and of form. If all priests are soldiers, missionaries are far more so. Many priests envy your vocation, but this is because they consider its magnificent ideal, rather than the daily monotony of a battlefield; they forget the reality of its self-sacrifice. Therefore, many of those who envy you from a distance would not dare to share your apostolate by working with you.

ENDURANCE

The second characteristic of a missionary's life is endurance. Yes! If it is a question of your own soul or the souls of others, you need great endurance to overcome interior trials and exterior difficulties successfully. Fortunately, you have a special call, and with it a special grace without which even the best wills would soon succumb. Is not this true? How I wish I could preach to you as if I had fought beside you in your hard battles.

Missionaries, and future missionaries, develop within you this great virtue of endurance so that you may triumph victoriously in the perilous hours when your heart is assailed. Develop this strength by increasing your personal love for the Heart of Jesus. It is only this divine fire which can give you the secret of resistance which is greater than any natural reserve of strength. Francis Xavier was the hero of a struggle which lasted ten years without intermission; Charles de Foucauld emulated him in another path of perfect self-immolation. Both of them were upheld by a love which rendered them invincible.

Notice especially that, however wonderful the endurance of the Curé of Ars, surrounded as he was by an admiring multitude, it is completely different from that of St. Francis Xavier. He was obliged to stand alone against difficulties which not only threatened to stop his work completely, but which tended to overthrow his own interior life by casting him into the depths of discouragement. Your case is that of St. Francis Xavier. Such is God's will, and therefore through love of Him and only through love of Him you must be ready to meet the difficulties and overcome them; for God's glory is at stake.

LOVE FOR SOULS

If it is true that people often admire your life, it is also true that they often pity you for having no home of your own, for being deprived of the affection of your relatives and for having to live far from your own people. Those who think this way have not looked into the heart of a missionary and therefore have no idea of one of the most beautiful and noble traits of your life. This trait is the intense, holy love that you have for the souls entrusted to your care, a love which attaches you to them by chains which only Divine Love can forge. You take root among your flock, and you feel so at home among them that it is a real sacrifice to have to leave them and go elsewhere, even if, from a natural point of view, the change would be an advantage and an honor.

It is an extraordinary grace not merely to be resigned but to give your heart to a people not your own according to nature, but who in the cross and for the sake of the adorable Crucified have become the object of your solicitude, of your devotedness even unto death. This is true even when, for long periods, you taste none of the consolations and rewards that you might expect and even lawfully seek. This is because you love your vocation without being deluded either by its poetry or its prose!

Whoever you are, whether missionaries of the East or West, North or South, may you be blessed a thousand times in thus consecrating all that is best in you — your heart and your strength — to the land that you water and render fruitful by the sweat of your brow, to the people of your adoption who have become your heritage of flowers and thorns, of bitterness and of joy. I know how you love this portion of the earth which is your parish, your district, which is for you a little portion of the promised Holy Land that you hope one day to sanctify by the supreme sacrifice — your death. May you indeed be blessed!

Love with an ever greater love this field which you have to clear and cultivate that it may bring forth blossom and fruit for our Lord; love this ground that is sometimes so barren, so ungrateful, so rebellious even against all your efforts; love it with a holy love which, like Jesus', will cause you to shed tears over it. The Precious Blood, and your tears and labors, will one day yield fruit a hundredfold for God's glory and yours.

JOY

All those who have been privileged to see you at your

95

work, to surprise you in the midst of your greatest moral or material difficulties, have been struck with the pure and overflowing joy which springs spontaneously from the heart of the missionary. This characteristic is so great and remarkable that, at first sight, it is apt to deceive. In seeing you always so happy and content, people are led to believe that you are exempt from all difficulty and care, that the work of spreading the Gospel is done, as it were, by magic, without great effort and always with astonishing success.

You know by experience that such is not the life of a true missionary. Yet in spite of frequent heavy crosses, your heart is full of incomparable peace and joy. It is rather like the perfect joy of St. Francis of Assisi which comes from the stripping of oneself, from the voluntary privation of many, even necessary things; a joy which comes from following our Lord closely, from seeking nothing but His love and His glory; a joy in fact which fills your heart in exchange for the weariness and trouble which you never count too great a price to pay for souls.

This intimate joy which belongs to all good missionaries is a divine caress and encouragement from the Lord who thus tells how greatly He is pleased with you even in the midst of your inevitable failures, in which you suffer in greater measure than He loses.

Cultivate in yourselves and among yourselves this holy joy which so lightens your burdens and replenishes your strength. Cherish and increase it for it is the exquisite flower of a great spirit of faithful and perfect abandonment to the divine Will. Sing a joyful hymn of thanksgiving because you are the pioneers of Christ's Gospel, the precursors of His Kingdom. Rejoice in advance at the glory which throughout eternity will be for you a heaven within your heaven. Each morning when standing at the altar, fill your heart with this living water, this pure and heavenly joy which is to spring up unto life eternal. Be the happy ones of this world, you who have willingly separated yourselves from so many things that you might enrich yourselves with the Heart of Jesus, and who for His sake enrich with truth and love those who sit in the darkness and shadow of death.

In this way you will prove the truth of words which might have been written especially for you: *"Now I rejoice in my sufferings"* (Col. 1:24).

ABANDONMENT

Lastly, I find the secret of your endurance and your joy especially in a virtue which best sums up all priestly and missionary virtues: a perfect abandonment of Divine Providence. It seems to me that you have become like sailors who are so used to the ocean, which is dangerous even when calm, that your peace never leaves you and you are always able to sleep. This is not because you are so used to danger and combat that you cease to feel them or are blinded by them. Far from it. Very often your horizon is dark and the waves threaten; but you have been formed in a splendid school of valiant courage — you have learned to confide always and in everything in a Providence that watches especially over missionaries, and therefore your peace never leaves you.

As a matter of fact, how many times in hours of peril, when humanly speaking all seemed lost, have you not strengthened and comforted each other with these simple words of supreme wisdom: "We abandon ourselves into the hands of a loving God"? Shipwreck — that is to say, the ruin of the dearest work of your life — seemed imminent, and suddenly an unlooked-for solution saved both the mission and the missionaries. And when the storm passed, how often a period of peace followed, during which a quite unexpected harvest of rich conversions was gathered in, so that you truly reaped in joy what you sowed in tears.

Steady your boat, which has to navigate such perilous waters, with the divine ballast of this complete abandonment to God. At all times, but especially during hours of anguish, it will fill you with a deep peace, and will keep perfect poise in the heart of every good missionary.

If the word "missionary," means "one sent," you must have a very great faith in Him who has sent you, and who, having sent you, knows what is necessary to accomplish His divine plan according to His Will, through the instrumentality of men and circumstances.

Therefore, you have a thousand reasons for remaining calm in the midst of storm. Do your duty. Do it, if necessary, even unto heroism. Never bargain with God. Live up to your glorious traditions, sparing neither strength nor weariness and sealing all by your blood if God so wills. But once your duty is accomplished, rest in complete abandonment to divine Providence; do not be too anxious; do not have any unreasonable fear of the wickedness of your enemies.

Peace and abandonment to God, for Divine Wisdom guides you! Peace and abandonment, for it is God Almighty who traces out your way! Peace and abandonment, for the love of God surrounds both you and all that you love in Him and for Him — your work and the souls of which you have care! *"With God on our side who can be against us?"* (Rom. 8:31).

Have unbounded peace, peace in a perfect abandonment to God. When the hour of supreme justice strikes "you will see the Son of Man seated at the right hand of the Power (Matt. 27:64). Calling you to receive the crown of eternal life, He will say to you: *"Today you will be with Me in Paradise"* (Luke 23:43).

10. Doctrine of the Sacred Heart of Jesus

Nothing is more suited to help us attain the two ideals of the priesthood — to be holy priests and successful apostles — than the doctrine of the Sacred Heart, when it is really understood according to the spirit and teaching of the Church.

How the great saints of other ages would have rejoiced in knowing the Heart of Jesus as we do today! More fortunate than they, we, who are living in the full splendor of the rays from that divine Sun — the Heart of Jesus —, should know how to profit fully from the light and fire pouring forth from this adorable Heart upon the Church and upon souls.

"O Mother of fair love, Queen of the Cenacle, open to us priests the sanctuary of the Sacred Heart! Teach us to enter into this furnace of divine love in order to obtain therein the burning love we need for our own sanctification, and to enkindle the flame of love for the Sacred Heart in the souls, the families, the parishes, God has entrusted to our care."

Let us now try to fathom what St. Paul calls "the breadth and length and height and depth" of the love of God, manifested to the world by the love of Jesus Christ.

Theologically speaking, what do we understand by the expression "the Heart of Jesus"? We do not mean only or principally His heart of flesh, which is worthy of adoration as is the whole divine Person. Under the symbol of a physical heart the Church teaches us the same doctrine taught by St. John: *"Deus caritas est"* — "God is love." Further, the fact that our Lord Jesus Christ is the God-Man, is the revelation of that infinite love which is God the Father: "I have loved you with an everlasting love" (Jer. 31:3).

Again, even as all the relations of God with His creatures begin and end in love and by love, so also, as creatures, all our relations with our Creator must, "through Jesus Christ," have their starting point and their completion in and by love.

Notice how this *Deus-Caritas* in giving Himself to us gives us only love, and likewise in exercising His rights over us, asks in return only for the love of His creatures. This led St. Paul to say "Love therefore is the fulfillment of the Law" (Rom. 13:10). To confirm and to accentuate this law of love, which embraces heaven and earth, the apostle breaks forth into the most astonishing and sublime passage in all his famous epistles: "If I should speak with the tongues of men and of angels, but do not have charity, I have become as sounding brass or a tinkling cymbal. And if I have prophecy and know all mysteries and all knowledge, and if I have all faith so as to remove mountains, yet do not have charity, I am nothing. And if I distribute all my goods to feed the poor, and if I deliver my body to be burned, yet do not have charity, it profits me nothing" (I Cor. 1-3).

In this sense — and it is the only doctrinal one — *"Cor Jesu"* is not a mere devotion in the ordinary and popular sense of the word but a wonderful synthesis of Catholic dogma and morals. This was the way a former archbishop of Poitiers explained to a young priest how he understood the theology of the Sacred Heart: "My dogma — *"He loved me. . ."* My morals — *"You shall love. . ."* — this is what I mean by *"Heart of Jesus."*

* * * * *

The doctrine of the Sacred Heart can be summed up in what I call "the Gospel of the Heart of Jesus" in three chapters.

The first chapter: because of His infinite, incomprehensible love God willed to redeem the guilty world. He might have done this in one of a thousand ways, each one worthy of His divine Majesty. But He chose the lowliest way of all, that of humiliation: *"And the Word became Flesh"* (John 1:14).

If a simple child or a learned theologian asks the why and the wherefore of this mystery there is but one answer — the only one that is enlightening, the only doctrinal one — the answer given by God Himself: *"For God so loved the World"* (John 3:16) — love!

Let us now turn the page to *the second chapter*. The Incarnation was more than enough to save a thousand worlds, and yet God willed to do more. He did not have to become incarnate, yet He was made man. Having accomplished this stupendous miracle, being God, He did not have to die, yet He willed to become a corpse: *"He was crucified. . .He died, and was buried"* (Creed). The astonished angels ask the "why" and "wherefore." For them as well as for us, the answer is the same: *"Sic Deus dilexit mundum."* The "folly of the cross" can be explained only by the excess and folly of a divine love.

The third chapter: before dying and returning to His Father, Christ determined not to leave us orphans. And so, on Holy Thursday, the Man-God of the Incarnation and of the cross gave Himself to us until the end of time in the Holy Sacrifice of the Mass and in the Blessed Sacrament.

Before you ask the "why" and the "wherefore," I forestall you and repeat the words which give us the key to this mystery: "Having loved His own who were in the world, He loved them unto the end." . . . *"For God so loved the world. . ."* The infinite charity of God; the love — and nothing but the infinite love — of Jesus Christ, is the only adequate explanation of this supreme gift of God.

Now, which one of these three chapters contains the true doctrine of the Sacred Heart? Is it the first, the Incarnation? Is the second, the Cross? Or is it the third, the Holy Eucharist? Obviously, we may prefer to meditate on or preach about one or another of these three marvelous mysteries, according to our personal devotion and attraction: "The Spirit breathes where He wills" (cf. John 3:8).

Thus in the annals of the Church we have a great number of saints who have been attracted especially by the Incarnation. An example would be St. Thérèse of Lisieux. Many others have been fascinated by the beauty of the cross; for instance, St. Francis of Assisi and St. John of the Cross. Still others have devoted their lives to loving the Blessed Sacrament, towards which they felt a special attraction. Among these we might mention St. Paschal Baylon, St. Eymard, or St. Juliana of Falconieri. In each instance these saints followed the inspiration of the Holy Spirit according to their special vocation.

But from the moment we speak of the *doctrine* of the Sacred Heart, and not of personal attraction and devotion, there will be no longer a question of one or another of the three chapters, but of *all three. Together* they form the integral Gospel of the love of God manifested by the Incarnation of the Word, by His Passion and death and by the incomparable gift of Himself in the Holy Eucharist. Thus the Summa Theologica contained in these words of St. John, "God is love," is not to be found in one chapter more than in another, but in the three fused into one. The "digest" of this marvelous Gospel of love is the pierced Heart of Jesus, surrounded by the symbols of His Passion.

* * * * *

If I were called upon to reproduce this doctrine in the form of a picture, I would present it as a triptych. In the center I would place St. Thomas Aquinas kneeling in adoration before the Blessed Sacrament, singing his marvelous Tantum Ergo. On the right would be St. Thérèse of the Child Jesus with arms outstretched towards the divine Babe of Bethlehem; on the left, Murillo's painting of Jesus crucified, embracing St. Francis of Assisi. In the center, also kneeling before the

Blessed Sacrament, we see St. Margaret Mary. Suddenly these three saints raise their eyes as though called by a mysterious voice. There above the altar they see our Lord as He appeared at Paray-le-Monial, His pierced Heart all on fire in the wound of His sacred side.

Then St. Margaret Mary bids the three of them to notice how they find in "this Heart which has so loved men," the mysteries each of them symbolizes: the humiliation of the Incarnation, the folly of the Cross, and the annihilation of the Eucharist, "Behold," she repeats, "this Heart which has so loved men." Joining my voice to hers I add: "Who would not love in return One who has loved us so much? In exchange for His love, our love; in exchange for His Heart, our hearts. 'My son, give Me thy heart.' "

As far as sublime and abstract ideas can be painted on canvas, I think this triptych sums up the doctrine of the Sacred Heart very clearly and exactly.

* * * * *

According to this reasoning, which combines doctrine and love, theory and life, I find the Heart of Jesus — that is to say, His love — in His entire adorable Person:

In His head crowned with thorns through love;

In His eyes which shed tears of love;

In His mouth which thirsted and spoke only words of love;

In His hands pierced through love;

In His feet transfixed through love;

In His side opened through love;

In His whole body which became a living wound of love.

Therefore with a saintly cardinal I repeat: "Jesus Christ whole and entire is nothing else but an infinite heart."

And just as His divine Person is love, so do all His works proclaim His love and claim ours in return: the creation, the redemption, the priesthood, the Holy Sacrifice, the tabernacle, grace, the communion of saints, and our Lady. Furthermore, Jesus tells us the entire law is comprised in two commandments, the love of God and neighbor; but the second is absolutely dependent upon and presupposes the first.

The Heart of Jesus, then, is the center from which emanate, as from a furnace of love, all the divine actions and toward which all things in the divine plan converge. It is logical therefore to conclude that the cult of the Heart of Jesus is not a mere chapter, or tract, but a complete *summary* of the most sublime doctrine. In this sense heaven will be an everlasting feast of the Sacred Heart.

* * * * *

It is evident that there is nothing new as far as the *doctrine* of the Sacred Heart is concerned — it is found in the revelations of the Gospel. But as regards the *form*, the external liturgical cult of the Sacred Heart, this is new, dating from the revelations of Paray-le-Monial.

Here is one example of what I call "new" in worship and form: the feast of the Sacred Heart, raised by Pope Pius XI to a feast of the first class, by Pope Paul VI to the rank of a Solemnity, and celebrated on the Friday following the octave (now suppressed) of the Feast of Corpus Christi, according to the explicit request of our Lord to St. Margaret Mary. *

Yes, we must never forget that the essential doctrine of the Heart of Jesus is the very substance of dogma itself. This is so true that we can affirm that in order to preach the doctrine of the Sacred Heart we have no need of St. Margaret Mary. The Gospel and our theology suffice. If, with the Church, I love and admire the great events of Paray it is because I find them to be in perfect harmony with the gospels, as regards their requests, their spirit and their promises.

Notice for example how the adorable Master returns to Paray with identically the same aim and plan as when He

*"The present devotion to the Sacred Heart, in spite of its continuity as far back as the Bible, has not always existed in the form in which it exists today (think for instance of the Church's liturgical cult of the Sacred Heart. . ." (**Heart of the Saviour**, Herder and Herder, p. 140)

came to Bethlehem, to Calvary and to our altars: to give love and to receive love; to conquer and draw hearts to His Heart. In Palestine and in Paray He suffers from the same thirst, the thirst for love. He came to earth twenty centuries ago and He appeared at Paray, for the same purpose, to enkindle a fire upon earth: "I have come to cast fire upon the earth, and would that it were already enkindled!" (Luke 12:49).

Yes, agreeing wholeheartedly with· the Church's verdict on the revelations at Paray-le-Monial, we can affirm that they had no other aim than to increase the knowledge and the spirit of our adoption as sons of God, stressing our relations with God through Jesus the Mediator, accentuating the principle of a love "strong as death," and reaffirming, as the foundation of the life of the soul and of its ascension to the Father and to the Blessed Trinity, the queen of all the virtues, love. This is the real meaning of those words addressed by our Lord to St. Margaret Mary, words that have now become a classic: "I will reign through My Heart!" He wishes to conquer, to triumph through charity, through love.

* * * * *

One last word on the *"nova et vetera"* of the doctrine of the Sacred Heart. St. Francis de Sales says most beautifully: "If an autopsy had been performed on the body of Jesus as is done with kings, it would have been discovered that the wound in the Heart of Jesus did not date from the blow of the lance on Calvary, but rather from the Incarnation — that Jesus was born with a wounded heart, a heart wounded by love."

Paray drew attention to the opened side so that we might enter therein and understand by meditation and prayer what St. Francis de Sales tells us, "if the wound made by the lance dates from yesterday, the lance only tore the curtain that we might see the wound of eternal love."

The Son of God came to earth primarily to reveal to us the love God has had for us from all eternity. He came to

Paray-le-Monial for the same reason: to remind us of this everlasting love and to plead for the love of our hearts in return.

Profit from this doctrinal devotion to the divine Heart of Jesus to develop your interior life, for your own benefit and for that of others. In this regard I call your attention to two promises of the Sacred Heart, to my mind the greatest of all those made at Paray. The first concerns priestly holiness: "Fervent souls shall rise speedily to great perfection." God is faithful, always and in all things, and especially so when it is a question of a cause above all others so dear to His Heart, the sanctification of His priests.

The second promise has to do with your *cura animarum:* "I will give to priests the power of touching the hardest hearts." If you wish to possess the true secret of converting the most obstinate sinners, if you wish to see a desert bloom for the glory of the Lord of the harvest, then take the triumphant standard of the Heart of Jesus, and enthrone Him as the loving King of souls, of homes, of your parish and of all your organizations; make this loving King the center of all hearts; preach His love and His mercy; be genuine apostles of His Sacred Heart.

One day not only your faith but also your experience will prove to you how great is His fidelity in keeping and even surpassing His promises in favor of priests, who like John, are friends and apostles of His pierced Heart. Ask the Mother of Fair Love to obtain for you the science of the saints *par excellence*, the one that comprises all others and without which they are useless: "The science of the love of Christ." For Jesus Himself has told us: "If anyone love me . . . my Father will love him and we will come to him and make our home with him." (cf. John 14:33).

Abide in His love, for "love is the fulfillment of the Law." "Thou shalt love . . . this is the first and the greatest of the commandments . . . My son, give Me thy heart." Love with a manly love the Heart of the God who loved you so much.

In addition to trust, the spirit of sacrifice and apostolic

zeal — those three great proofs of your love — your daily Mass must be the hearth at which to enkindle the love which is so necessary for your personal sanctification and the sanctification of others.

Utilize the solid doctrine of the Sacred Heart to strengthen between your heart and His that bond of intimate friendship which He longs to see established between Himself and His priests.

It was not in vain that the Savior explicitly promised to "raise to a high degree of perfection the faithful disciples of His adorable Heart." No priest worthy of the name would want to bypass such a marvelous blessing. Yours is the privilege of taking the place of St. John, the beloved disciple. It is yours by right, because you are priests. It was on the same Heart, whose beatings were heard by John at the Last Supper, that have been formed the saints, missionaries and martyrs. For, once again, devotion to the Sacred Heart of Jesus, is not "a" devotion but a *life of love:* the practice of that manly virtue which is the queen of virtues and which sums up all the rest, "the science of the love of Christ."

Become a part of this movement which is a veritable breath of the Holy Spirit, flooding the Church with light and fire. Under the slogan of "Most Sacred Heart of Jesus, Thy Kingdom Come!" it has become the inspiration and motivating force of all modern apostolates.*

Do all in your power to make Jesus' love better known and loved, for even among the good, it is so little known. Strengthen their faith, yes, but at the same time increase their love of our Lord, give them His Heart. Otherwise you run the risk of forming lukewarm Catholics lacking love for the Eucharist and the spirit of sacrifice and zeal.

Catholics who believe are to be found everywhere, but far too many have only a spark of love, and some, none at

---

*"It is likewise our most fervent desire that all who profess themselves Christians and are seriously engaged in the effort to establish the Kingdom of Christ on earth will consider the practice of devotion to the Heart of Jesus the source and symbol of unity, salvation and peace." (Pope Pius XII, **Haurietis Aquas**, #122, Sacred Heart Publication Center, Orlando, Florida 32806)

all. It was this lack of love on the part of His friends that occasioned the bitter complaints of our Lord at Paray. As Pope Pius XI stated in his encyclical on reparation, this is the origin of the practices of reparation now widespread in the Church, such as the Holy Hour, First Friday Communions of reparation, and the great feast of the Sacred Heart.

For your part, fulfill generously all the requests made by the Sacred Heart and which have been seconded by the Church, and one day you will learn from a happy experience how royally faithful He is to His promises.

For I desired mercy
(Osee 6:6).

11. Merciful Love

Many long years of preaching to the clergy, both diocesan and regular, have profoundly convinced me that we priests, even more than the faithful, badly need a great deal of encouragement which I call "moral oxygen" for the heart. Why? Because the struggle for priestly perfection is always rugged and rough, and the path is strewn with a thousand obstacles from within and without.

Again, even among the best of us, reserves of energy and good will are quickly used up, and we do not always see the ground gained or the progress made. On the other hand, our faults and failings stare us in the face.

If this is true of our interior life, what are we to say of that other battle in which we are engaged, the battle to do good, to save souls, to maintain the ground won so painfully, and to push on to new victories for the Master? How many combined circumstances there are that seem to be opposing our work: lack of personnel, of resources, of health, of encouragement. There are times when we seem to be overwhelmed by feelings of depression and discouragement.

Perhaps this happned to you yesterday, or maybe you are facing a similar crisis today. In any case, to strengthen and encourage you, allow me to say to you as did the angel to the prophet: "Arise and eat, else the journey will be too great for you" (I Kings 19:7).

What is this food at once so palatable and so strengthening and so necessary for the priest and missionary? It is the doctrine of mercy. Believe me, it is the Heart of Jesus Himself who prepared this bread for you, and He gives it to you not only during the retreat but for your entire life. "Take and eat" without limit for the adorable Master has told us: "I desire mercy" (Matt. 9:13).

*****

First of all, are the words mercy and love equivalent terms? Not always! For instance, the fallen angels were created through God's wisdom and love, but they never experienced His mercy. After having been masterpieces of His love they became demons.

On the other hand, man, likewise created by God's wisdom and love, was ransomed by the mercy of the same God who became man and died to save him. This is the reason the devil cried out in despair during an exorcism, "Why did you receive mercy after your sin and not I?"

Only those who have been baptized in the Blood of our Savior will be able to say in heaven, "With Your Blood You purchased for God men of every race and nation" (Rev. 5:9), while the angels will have to adore in silence.

The longer I preach, the more this doctrine becomes an obsession with me, because the older you get the more you understand that your faults are due almost always to weakness, and rarely to malice. This means that everyone needs mercy: the saints, because they know they cannot rely on the weak reed of human nature; the large army of those struggling to sanctify themselves, who therefore know their need of conversion.

I have never regretted having preached this doctrine in season and out of season and to all types of souls. Everywhere I have been overwhelmed with surprises — surprises that would be wonderful were it not for the sad fact that they revealed, even in the very sanctuary itself, the presence of living corpses that divine mercy alone was capable of resurrecting.

* * * * *

What is the meaning of mercy according to the Gospel? It signifies a divine predilection for the weak, for the sick, for the abandoned, for the despised and the outcasts. In order to discover Jesus it was only necessary to seek out the sinners or the downtrodden: there He could always be found.

Oh, the wonderful scandal of the Savior openly seeking the company of the publicans, even asking them for hospitality and offering them, together with His friendship, the honor of being associated with His work of salvation! In Zacchaeus and Levi we find the personification of a system inaugurated by Jesus and which was an unheard of innovation. What prophet could say as He did, "The Son of Man came to seek and to save what was lost" (Luke 19:10)?

This special love for the lost sheep of the flock is so outstanding that the parable of the prodigal son expressly brings out the indignation and jealousy of the older son who remained faithful. He had nothing to complain about, everything belonged to him. But the Heart of God the Savior was reaffirming His right to celebrate a great banquet in heaven in honor of the repentant sinner, rather than for the ninety-nine just who persevered. Needless to say, since then this familiar doctrine is always new and up-to-date.

For instance, I have known the case of a priest who, because of his weakness, badly needed mercy, but who resisted all the attempts of the Good Shepherd to bring him back. Finally, after many long years, he was captured by the infinite mercy of the Heart of Jesus, the only possible explanation for such a conversion. You should have seen the old priest weeping tears of joy, of sorrow and of gratitude! We cannot repeat too often that Jesus was, and always will be, above all else, a Savior for those He has redeemed. By this I mean that here below, *in via*, en route to our heavenly home, Jesus is more a patient, kind and merciful Savior than a terrible and severe Judge. That is why He waits ten, twenty, fifty years or more, in order to show mercy, even though it be at the eleventh hour.

*****

Never forget, never tone down the strong and consoling doctrine of mercy found on every page of the Gospel. When we stand before the divine tribunal strict and rigorous justice will be meted out to us. In the meantime, along the way, we will find the Heart of a Savior-God who wants us to have life, and life in abundance. *"Copiosa apud eum redemptio"* (Ps. 129:7).

There is another aspect of mercy: an offended God takes the first step towards His ungrateful sons, become His executioners. He pleads with them, He begs them to be willing to receive His forgiveness; to spare Him the sorrow of having to punish them.

Yes, the initiative for every reconciliation between the sinner and Christ, whom he crucified, has always been taken by the Victim. The unanswerable, the overwhelming argument for all this is the Incarnation. The Word *"For us men and for our salvation He came down from Heaven"* (Creed).

It is a remarkable fact that Sacred Scripture nowhere mentions a word about guilty Adam imploring forgiveness: on the contrary it is an offended God who offers it to him the very day of the fall. And so the Father sends His only Son in pursuit of sinners. Ever since then it is the story of the Good Shepherd looking for the lost sheep.

It is impossible to imagine peace on earth or in heaven apart from God. We cannot do without Him. And yet by sin we leave Him, we eliminate Him from our lives. He is the Supreme Being who has no need of His creatures and even less so when His subjects rebel and are knowingly guilty of sin.

But here is the unfathomable mystery: It is precisely this God of Majesty who, because of His thirst for my love and His desire for my happiness, forgets my ingratitude, comes to meet me, to conquer me with the treasures of

His tenderness and His mercy. This is a wonderful and beautiful doctrine, but even greater are the miracles which confirm it.

For instance, I had enthroned the Sacred Heart of Jesus in the home of a bitter enemy of the Church. He had tolerated the ceremony out of politeness and love for his family. After a great deal of prayer and assurance from the members of his family that they would be frequent communicants and fervent apostles of the Sacred Heart, I decided on a plan which at that time seemed a foolish provocation. With no claim whatever to his friendship I wrote him a note, telling him in the name of the Sacred Heart to meet me the following Friday in order to make his confession.

It was really Jesus seeking out His enemy!

What a wonderful surprise it was for me and for his family when, at the appointed time, he arrived prepared to make a good confession. To be sure his feelings would not get the best of him, he had written down his sins, which he read with every mark of true contrition. The following day during my Mass he made his first Holy Communion at the age of seventy!

The joy in Heaven, predicted by our Lord, must have been indescribable.

* * * * *

Mercy sometimes means a long and fearsome struggle for the Good Shepherd to reclaim a lost sheep fighting to escape. One would think this soul were the apple of His eye, so great is His desire to win it for heaven. Not satisfied with the miracle of his cross, He multiplies marvelous stratagems in order to conquer His prey. And the more ungrateful and guilty the sinner, the greater His efforts.

An example: I knew a clerical prodigal son who had attempted marriage. He had made up his mind to steel himself against grace, under the pretext of old age and a false sense of loyalty. I can still see him, fighting desperately for four days against grace. But the merciful

Heart of Jesus was stronger than he, and he finally had the courage to break his bonds. He left without even getting his personal effects. He is dead now, and in heaven must be "singing the mercies of the Lord forever!"

We have cost Him so much! For this reason, and because He knows our weakness so well, Jesus forgives easily.

Another mysterious quality of divine mercy is the simplicity with which an offended God pardons His guilty creatures. Not a word was spoken by Mary Magdalene; the woman taken in adultery was dragged unwillingly to the feet of Jesus; the paralytic did not ask for pardon, but sought only a physical cure. The same was true of the blind man whose healing caused such a stir. In each of them our Lord saw the depths of their sins, but he also saw their unexpressed sorrow, and so to all of them he said the same thing: "Thy sins are forgiven thee, go in peace and sin no more." This is why He came to earth: to show forth the goodness and the mercy of His Father, of whom He is the substantial Splendor.

So great was the novelty of this doctrine of mercy, that in the early days of the Church some of the Gospel stories of His forgiveness of great sinners were suppressed.

* * * * *

What else is the wonderful and often forgotten dogma of the Communion of Saints but a marvelous proof of divine mercy? Mercy is the only explanation for the fact that you and I are permitted to pay each other's debts, thereby saving one another from the punishment of hell.

Why did God not force the guilty sinner to pay his own debts contracted by his sins? We find Him doing just the opposite. His infinite mercy, which has foreseen every detail of our lives, which is constantly hovering around us, is determined that we shall be saved at any cost. Over and over again, it is the story of the arms of the Good Shepherd pressing the prodigal son, the lost sheep, to His Heart, offering complete pardon and an eternity of happiness in heaven.

The price of these miracles of mercy and salvation is the countless sacrifices and prayers of that army of living victims whose self-immolation is the most glorious of apostolates. St. Teresa of Avila was a soul of this stamp; more recently and even more evidently, St. Thérèse of Lisieux, that wonderful missionary of love. Following their example, thousands of other hidden apostles continue to people heaven with the souls they save through their prayers and sacrifices. How often an act of pure love, a sacrifice, has won the grace of salvation for a dying sinner, perhaps about to be plunged into hell!

We priests should never forget that our own vocation is an act of mercy shown to us by our Lord. Let it always be a canal through which floods of mercy pour out on souls entrusted to our care. We are proofs that the Master never abandons the sinner, the prodigal son, the lost sheep, but rather seeks him out wherever he may be. Priests are living reproductions of Him whom the Father sent into the world for the salvation of those who live in the shadow of death. "As the Father has sent me so also I send you." We are living proofs and perfect examples of the doctrine, "I will have mercy. . . ." The priest preaches mercy and he shows mercy. This being so, you can expect to receive mercy in abundance both in life and in death. "Blessed are the merciful, for they shall obtain mercy" (Matt. 5:7).

In your hours of difficulty, in the face of obstacles that discourage you and cause you to lose confidence; when Satan tries to discourage you by pointing out your weaknesses and exaggerating your deficiencies; especially when he tries to convince you that all your efforts to sanctify yourself and others are a waste of energy, then is the time to hold fast to the solid doctrine of blind confidence in the merciful love of the Heart of Jesus.

Yes, preach divine mercy to others, but above all apply this consoling doctrine to yourself. By so doing you will please the Heart of Jesus; He will supply for what is wanting in you and will preserve your soul "unto life everlasting."

* * * * *

For a priest who *lives* the doctrine of mercy, there is no problem in believing in it. But we cannot stop there. We must hand it on to others, in the confessional, in the pulpit, and whenever we come in contact with souls, with their thousand and one problems. Explain often to them that wonder of mercy, their baptism. Stir up their zeal for the salvation of others by giving them a clear picture of the meaning of the dogma of the Communion of Saints, that outstanding proof of divine mercy. Let this limitless treasure of grace be for them a stimulus to work for the conversion of those who do not have the gift of faith or for those who have lost it.

Most Sacred Heart of Jesus, burning with love for me, inflame my heart with love for Thee!

I know whom I have believed
(II Tim. 1:12).

12. Confidence!

Lake Genesareth is still shrouded in cloudy darkness. Suddenly, as the disciples struggle against the storm, Jesus comes walking to them upon the water. They fail to recognize Him, and are seized with terror, taking Him for a phantom. Suddenly, they hear these reassuring words, "Fear not . . . it is I."

What doctrinal truths are contained in these few words of the Master! "Fear not." Why? Because, "It is I." (If I were an angel, a prophet, even a saint, you would have reason to fear, for none of these could know you through and through as I do. Above all not one of them can offer you infinite mercy and forgiveness. But, because "it is I," Jesus, you have nothing to fear. Place all your trust in Me!)

* * * * *

How badly we priests need the doctrine of confidence! "Once he finds himself in the ranks of the combatants," wrote Cardinal Manning of England, "no priest has any reason to fear."

Yet because of our terrific responsibilities, resulting from our duty of saving souls, we sometimes think we have found a pretext for giving in to discouragement. Add to this the daily realization of our weakness, and our lack of trust often does seem justified.

Certainly we have to be practical and be reminded, or remind ourselves, of the dangers we incur by neglecting our duties and otherwise trifling with grace. Some retreat masters and writers, however, seem to go too far, driving priests further down into the slough of despondency rather than giving them the encouragement they need and deserve. We must always counterbalance the dark side of the picture with the doctrine that alone is capable of imparting new supernatural energy, the doctrine of confidence. Side by side with the abyss of our miseries we must place the deeper abyss of divine mercy. If our wretchedness is great, we must likewise clearly state that the remedy — mercy — is infinite and its source close at hand.

How can a priest be a good Samaritan to others, if he himself is weighed down by his own shortcomings, is helpless to react against them, and drags himself along because of his lack of trustful love?

* * * * *

First of all, confide blindly in the infinite *wisdom* of Him who alone knows how to draw good from evil, health and strength from illness, and life from death itself. Have such a tremendous faith in the *wisdom* of God, that you let Him do with you whatever He wants. Allow Him to work out His plans as He wills, to the extent of going against your own plans, overthrowing your own projects, even though they be, as far as you can see, for His honor and glory.

Trust in His divine wisdom, which never destroys except to rebuild with eternity in view; which never sends a trial except to give peace and joy to the soul that He permits to suffer.

Trust in the divine Wisdom that has mysterious plans which escape our comprehension. "For my thoughts are not your thoughts; neither are your ways my ways, says the Lord" (cf. Is. 55:8).

When I was a young priest in Valparaiso, Chile, after much begging and hard work, I succeeded in building a

118

law school. Three months after its dedication in 1906, an earthquake leveled it to the ground. At the time I was tempted to ask, "Why? Why did You allow this to happen? This was for You and Your glory." But I did not, and today I know the reason God permitted this catastrophe. Had it not been for the earthquake I would not have had the great privilege of becoming a world-wide preacher of the merciful love of the Sacred Heart.

What marvels are being accomplished daily by God's wisdom! Only in eternity will they be unfolded before our astonished eyes. Then we shall clearly see the orderly course of events great and small, events permitted or willed, now inexplicable puzzles but in heaven seen as part of God's wonderful plan.

Eternity will be all too short to thank and praise this infinite Wisdom which, without ever consulting us, so often went against our ideas and projects, causing us suffering and sorrow only that we might be happy in heaven. Like little children we often rebelled, but there the purpose and tenderness of these seeming cruelties will be made clear. How well will we understand the wisdom and folly of the cross, and the unreasonable folly of our arguments, our calculations, our poor human wisdom! Perhaps if our Lord had permitted us to carry out our plans, we might have been lost forever.

This is what the Sacred Heart had in mind when He said to St. Margaret Mary, "Give Me a free hand . . . let Me do what I please." In these words we will find our security, our merit and our peace.

I once had to change trains going from Lourdes to Paris. By mistake I got aboard the wrong train. By the time I found out my error, my train had left. Naturally I felt annoyed, for it meant I would arrive many hours late for a retreat. But when I saw the next day's paper, I realized what a providential mistake it was. The train I should have taken never arrived in Paris; it was wrecked in a terrible accident, in which many were killed and injured.

We have all had similar experiences. They should teach us never to get upset if things turn out differently from the way we had planned. Never ask for explanations. Simply trust blindly the One who loves us and who permits many mysterious things to happen to us, because He loves us. Always take Jesus' "train" and you cannot make a mistake!

* * * * *

A second source of peace and confidence is the infinite *justice* of God, that justice so extraordinarily beautiful and so badly understood, so reassuring yet so calumniated, even by educated Catholics. How many there are who look upon it as synonymous with punishment and hell!

It is all too common to attribute damnation to justice and salvation to merciful love. Yet the truth is there are as many souls in heaven because of God's justice as because of His love.

Too often we forget that precisely because God is just He must be tender and bountiful. That wonderful little theologian St. Thérèse understood this when she wrote, "I trust His justice as much as I do His love."

Quite the contrary was the statement of a converted sinner, who in his happiness at being restored to the friendship of a God from whom he had expected nothing but punishment, made this classical remark to me: "Fortunately for me, God is *unjust* — otherwise I wouldn't be here!"

Yes, fortunately for us, we shall all one day be judged, not by an unjust judge, but by a Judge of infinite justice, who knows and weighs all the evidence; who, unlike men, is able to distinguish between ignorance, weakness and malice; who, consequently, never makes a mistake. His decisions are always just because they are based on infinite wisdom.

This infinitely just Judge cannot demand of a fledgling what He expects of an eagle. That is why, to the astonishment and even scandal of certain severe, ignorant or hypocritical minds, Jesus pardons great sinners far more easily than does the most loving of mothers. He knows us far better than our own mothers know us.

What surprises await us in Heaven! Remember the three great surprises enumerated by Gregory the Great! The first, "I am in Heaven!" What a surprise for those who feared God's justice so much. The second, the fact that some soul you thought so pious, so saintly, "hasn't arrived yet!" The third, when you see someone you did not like on earth, "What are *you* doing here?" What a surprise!

How I love St. Paul's words on this subject, words inspired by deep conviction: "There is laid up for me a crown of justice, which the Lord, the just Judge, will give to me on that day" (II Tim. 4:8). Notice that St. Paul does not appeal to the Savior of Mercy but to the Judge of infinite Justice, claiming the crown He has promised and which, he says, He owed him in strict justice.

Had St. Paul forgotten his violent persecution of and hatred for Christians? Had he forgotten his past sins? Not at all. Because he believed with a firm faith in the pardon promised to him ("but I obtained the mercy of God because I acted ignorantly, in unbelief" [I Tim. 1:13]), he did not hesitate to claim his reward.

How few Catholics — even priests — reason this way! Many look back over their lives and worry over past sins; by their attitude they seem to doubt God's pardon, and thus offend both the justice and the mercy of God.

This deplorable and dangerous frame of mind is due to a certain Jansenistic spirit which is quite widespread. Jansenism, which dries up the heart and freezes the blood, is rooted in a hidden pride; it is still the worst of heresies for it has succeeded principally in deceiving many of the leaders among the elite.

Years ago, when preaching in England, a bishop said to me, "Father, the nuns to whom you are going to preach have the reputation of never smiling. If you can change this Jansenistic spirit it will be the greatest thing yoiu have ever done."

On my way to the convent I wondered what I could do to break the ice. I hit upon a scheme. As soon as the sad looking portress opened the door I told her to inform Reverend Mother I wished to speak to the entire community in the chapter room at once. Sister was to take me there immediately. Startled though she was by this unusual request, she left to carry out my instructions.

Standing in the back of the chapter room I watched the nuns file in, one by one. They were indeed a sad looking group, and the saddest of all was the Reverend Mother.

When all were assembled, I pretended to want to leave, saying I had made a mistake, that I was told by the bishop I was going to preach to a community of *sisters*. "Well, what do you think we are?" demanded the superior, rising to the bait.

Then I struck home. "You are not *sisters*, you are a community of *war widows* mourning the loss of your husbands!"

The startled sisters raised their eyes in surprise. Then someone laughed and soon the entire group burst out laughing. Seizing the opening I proceeded then and there to give them a badly needed lesson on joy and happiness, on trust and confidence in religious life.

Later the bishop told me, "That is one of the greatest miracles I have ever heard of!"

* * * * *

The third reason we should trust the Sacred Heart of Jesus is because of His infinite *love* for us.

Rare indeed are those who can say with St. John, "And we have come to know, and have believed, the love that God has in our behalf" (I John 4:16). Truly we can say, "He came unto His own, and His own knew Him not" (John 1:11).

Yet God is nothing but love; Jesus is love. When He commands, when He forbids, when He rewards, when He corrects, when He punishes, it is always the Heart of Jesus manifesting itself. Even the severity which God sometimes displays here on earth is only the proof of His infinite mercy. It is His Heart chastising in time, that He may save in eternity. That is why rigorous justice in this world is in reality infinitely tender and merciful, for it often spares us a terrible purgatory and even hell itself.

Here is an example. A priest was severely punished by his bishop even though his guilt was not fully proved. Everyone agreed the punishment was too severe and friends of the priest all feared a violent reaction. But the excessive severity proved to be a boon. It opened his eyes, he acknowledged his wrong, accepted his penance, and made reparation for the harm he had done. He became a fervent priest and often thanked the divine mercy that inspired the severity of the bishop.

In our own case, is it not true that as we look back, our physical and moral trials, the bitterness we often had to suffer, the contradictions we have met with, have all been permitted by divine Providence, and have proved to be blessings in disguise, gifts of the loving Heart of Jesus?

You will never make a mistake when in your darkest and most painful hours, whether it is a question of your own interior life or your work for souls, you show a blind and unshakeable trust in the Heart of Jesus. Under the guise of virtue you can fear to excess, but you can never exaggerate the trust and confidence that go hand in hand with love and humility. In fact, it is precisely because you acknowledge your weakness and helplessness, which is true humility, that you should have such childlike trust in the Heart of Jesus. "I know whom I have *believed.*"

* * * * *

The loving confidence I urge you to have is not a virtue for saints confirmed in grace, but rather for those striving to become holy, who are fully conscious of the *"fomes peccati"* — their potentiality for sinning. Trustful love, or loving confidence, is above all for the weak who want to become strong, for those who know their own sinfulness by painful experience, but who in their humility sincerely wish to react against the current of human nature that would drag them down. For your encouragement, keep in mind that eighty-five per cent of the saints were penitents!

St. Thérèse of the Child Jesus understood this doctrine. As she so admirably put it:

"It is not because I have been preserved from mortal sin that I go to God with confidence and love. I feel that even if I had committed all possible crimes, I should lose nothing of my trust; but with a heart broken with sorrow and repentance I would throw myself into the arms of my Savior. I know how He cherished the prodigal son; I have heard His words to Mary Magdalen, to the woman taken in adultery, and to the Samaritan woman. No, no one would be able to frighten me, for I know what to expect from His love and mercy."

In other words, have boundless confidence in the Sacred Heart, *not in spite of but because of* your wretchedness.

Jesus is our Savior; He is our Physician, our Good Samaritan; He is the Good Shepherd. All these titles suppose on His part divine pity and infinite mercy; on our side, weakness and faults. He Himself has affirmed that "those that are well do not need a physician, but those that are sick."

In the course of my many long years of preaching I have had some very striking confirmations of this doctrine. One of them was the case of a nun who had the privilege of having our Lord as her director. The bishop asked me to talk to her a number of times. Apparently the case was genuine because of her humility and obedience.

One day after Communion the nun was crying. "Why are you crying?" asked our Lord. She answered, "Because this morning I saw myself for the first time as I really am." "And what are you?" asked Jesus. "I am nothing but a miserable rag!" Then came this wonderful answer: "If you are a miserable rag, take courage, place your trust in Me, for I am the divine Rag-picker!"

Yes, dear Fathers, He is just that, for were He not a divine Rag-picker, you and I would not be priests!"

If you would please Jesus, then, tell Him that you will keep your peace in the midst of the most violent storms; that you will acknowledge always and everywhere the reassuring and perfect harmony that exists between His justice, His wisdom and His infinite love.

And add with the psalmist: "In thee, O Lord, have I hoped, let me never be confounded" (Ps. 30:2).

* * * * *

The older I get the more convinced I become that we priests are not always the effective instruments of grace God wants us to be, because of our lack of confidence! If this is your case, remedy it by fighting the battle of your sanctification without ever retreating because of pessimism or discouragement. Be fearless in your ministry to souls, sustained by unshakeable trust. Stir it up especially in times of crisis, when overwhelmed with work, or stopped short by setbacks.

When, humanly speaking, you feel like doubting, that is the time to make an act of absolute faith in the wisdom, justice and love of our Lord. Hold your lines, advance, battle against the current, for if God is with you, and the Heart of Jesus is in your own heart, who can possibly have any success against you? That is the time to prove that these magnificent words were written for you: *"And so we know and believe the love God has for us"* (I John 4:16).

> *Most Sacred Heart of Jesus, burning with love for me, inflame my heart with love for Thee!*
>
> *Most Sacred Heart of Jesus, I place my trust in Thee!*

13. The Primacy of Love

Someone has written: According to Christian ideals, St. Paul is greater than the philosophers of Greece, and the blood of martyrs more sacred than the ink of the learned. This does not mean that thought is not divine, but that love is even more divine than thought. Thought inaugurates — love achieves. Only when faith blossoms into charity does it become enlightened and operative.

Far more profound, though, are these words of St. Paul: *"Love is the fulfilling of the Law."* This means that the perfection of the law and of all virtue, the perfection and full realization of Christian and priestly holiness, is love. As in heaven, so here below: the queen of virtues, the only everlasting virtue, is love.

Never forget that it is possible to believe without loving; that, unfortunately, faith and charity can be separated and in practice very often are. One can have faith — even a very lively faith — and yet have only a faint spark of charity, if even that. St. Paul tells us that faith and all the other gifts are useless without charity.

All priests have faith but all do not love sufficiently. That is why our faith and our hope grow weak; they are not being nourished by the strengthening food of love.

Only in a saint do we find perfect harmony between these two great virtues, for a saint loves with a boundless love what he believes, and he adores with an intense faith what he loves. That is why the "scientia caritatis Christi"

126

has always been the secret and the science of the saints. For what is holiness save living through God and in God, and with God who is in us? But God is nothing but love.

Here is a very simple truth, but one which is rarely thought about: God created us only through love that we might love Him in time and in eternity. This is the essence of the Good Tidings of the Gospel and its novelty. Pagan philosophers had arrived at the knowledge of the existence and nature of God, but only Jesus Christ made known to an astonished world that God is a Father of incomparable goodness and tenderness; that we are really His children and that He desires to be loved. This is what St. Paul calls the "era of grace." Ever since this revelation of our adoption as sons in Jesus Christ there has been a new spirit in our attitude toward God; "Let us pray with confidence to the Father in the words our Savior gave us."

This is the reason our Lord affirms that the first and the greatest commandment is *"Thou shalt love the Lord thy God."* But the stupendous facts of the Incarnation, the Redemption and our priesthood oblige us to love this God who is all love far more than the commandment. As St. Augustine tells us, *"Who would not love in return the One who loves us so much?"*

Add to this a personal motive for loving our Lord: all that is good in you, everything you are, all that you have received from the time of your baptism through your ordination to this very moment, your entire personal history, as God alone knows it, is nothing else but a miracle of merciful love. If this is true, then each of us should be a "miracle" of grateful love. That is why God's love presses you and surrounds you like a consuming flame: *"The love of Christ impels us!"*

* * * * *

After all that has been said, it is evident that great attention must be paid to the formation of *priestly hearts.* I stress the phrase "priestly hearts" to bring out the

127

necessity of teaching future priests to love God and His Son, whom He has sent.

The training of the intellect is certainly necessary and even indispensable. But this alone is not enough. Undoubtedly religion is truth and light, but it must be a truth lived through love.

Knowledge and love will be all one in Heaven, but here below they may be, and often are, separated. If it is true in general that *instruction* is not *education*, how much more true is it that a priest may receive a splendid intellectual formation and yet one which leaves his heart far from the ideal of holiness appropriate to his state of life?

There are plenty of specialists in the art of subtle speculation, theological and otherwise, but unfortunately saints are lacking because they do not live up to these fine principles. And the reason is obvious: they do not love. That is what the author of *Imitation of Christ* had in mind when he wrote: "It is better to love the Blessed Trinity than to write learned dissertations about the Trinity." How often do we not find mediocrity in virtue, devotedness and zeal among those who are versed in the knowledge of the "scientia sine caritate!" For the total and integral formation of the priest more is needed than the cold artificial light of electric bulbs. What we need is the light and fire, the knowledge and love of the Sun!

In expressing my sincere convictions on this subject, please do not think I am alluding to mere sensible love or still less to a vague sentimentality — far from it! I have in mind, on the contrary, that love "strong as death" which does not consist of feelings and words but in knowing how and being willing to sacrifice self after the example of the Master, who "loved me and delivered Himself for me." It is because too little importance is attached to this fundamental doctrine of love that often we build upon sand — the foundation is weak.

For instance, in the formation of seminarians and priests, stress is rightly laid upon mortification, humility, chastity and zeal. This is good. But it is not enough. Too often not enough emphasis is placed on the one and only thing that can develop all these priestly virtues: the love of our Lord Jesus Christ.

As a matter of fact, who will be more mortified than he who is deeply in love with Jesus crucified, and therefore, with His Cross?

Who will be truly humble to the point of dying to himself, of loving humiliations, except the one who is an intimate friend of the divine Heart of Jesus who said, "Learn of me, for I am meek and humble of heart"?

Who will be chaste in mind and heart if not he who has filled his heart and life with a divine love which shuts out all unlawful earthly affections?

Who will be more eaten up with zeal for souls than the priest who has exchanged his heart for the Heart of the Savior and who, because of his burning love, can say with St. Paul: "I will most gladly spend and be spent myself for your souls" (II Cor. 12:15)?

And who will really and truly love his brethren more than he who has a strong personal love for God?

In the light of all this, I think I understand why our Lord's sole complaint at Paray-le-Monial was that *He was not loved*. He had every right to complain of want of faith, of the spirit of sacrifice, of generosity. Still He only spoke about the lack of love. Why? Because when this is missing, everything else is missing. When we love but little or wrongly, the spiritual life within us dies out: "Qui non diligit manet in morte" (I John 3:14).

Make love the cornerstone of the foundation of your spiritual life; let it be the soul of your apostolic zeal. In season and out of season meditate on this most divine of eternal truths: God is love and our baptism and our priesthood oblige us before all else to give Him total love in return, loving Him *with all your heart, with all your soul, with all your strength.*

Love — love with a boundless love that your priestly work may be fruitful, that it may really give glory to God and be a source of grace for souls and for yourself. "It is God who gives the increase" and "God is love."

Love — love with a boundless love that self-sacrifice may become sweet and the cross of your vocation light, that your self-immolation may be a source of priestly sanctity for you and of supernatural life for others. To this end, *suffer through love and love through suffering*. Love is self-immolation!

Love — love with a boundless love in reparation for the shortcomings of your priestly life, to fill up what is wanting in you, to make up for what you have failed to give to God and souls. Remember "Charity covers a multitude of sins!" Love is reparation!

Finally, love — love with a boundless love, that the lamps of your hearts may be ready and burning when the Lord comes to render to each one according to his works. Love is heaven!

But if, on seeing Him at that hour, you are troubled and fearsome, may He Himself reassure you with His own words: *"Peace to you. . .do not be afraid. . .It is I!"* (cf. John 6:20; Luke 24:36).

And if, in your humility, thinking always of your failures you reply with a justifiable filial fear: "Lord, what about my many shortcomings, my defects, my sins and my responsibilities? . . . Jesus, how can I help but fear in the presence of my Judge?" may Christ be able to console and calm you with a tender smile and with words that will enable you to expect a merciful judgment: "My friend, my priest, all that you recognize as imperfect in your life is true. But, My peace be with you!"

"But why, Lord?"

"Because you have loved much! You have loved Me much and you have been the apostle of My love . . . Peace!"

Then in your last agony, resting on the Heart of your Savior, you will say to Him, if not in words at least with each beat of your heart: "I have found the Heart of a King, I have found the Heart of a Brother, I have found the Heart of a Friend, O most kind Jesus! O how good and how sweet it is to live and die in this Heart! It is good for me to be here forever!"

Only one is your Teacher, the Messiah (Matt. 23:10).

14. Love that You May Understand

The words applied to St. John, our Lord's precursor, *"He was the lamp, set a flame and burning bright"* (John 5:35), should be true of every priest. Because of his mission, he should be a burning flame of love to enkindle love in the hearts of others and at the same time a burning light to enlighten and guide those whom God has entrusted to his care.

When love is not merely a spark — ordinary virtue — but an ardent flame, it always gives off a strong light which, rising from the heart of the priest to his mind, becomes for him a vital element of supernatural knowledge. Hence this axiom well-known to the saints: "Ama et cognosces — love and you will understand." This means simply: love God fervently and He will reward your love by manifesting Himself to you. Love your Savior, and His Heart, touched by your love, will reveal secrets reserved for His intimate friends.

So often we are told: "To know God is to love Him." This is a necessary prerequisite in the philosophical order: *"Nothing is willed unless it is first known."* But it is only the first step: "Know Me that you may love Me." The second *supernatural* step towards perfection is: "Love Me that you may know Me . . . intimately."

This is what our Lord said to St. Angela of Foligno: "He who loves in fire will know in charity."

Therefore I repeat: the flames of ardent love generate

an extraordinary light in the order of divine and supernatural knowledge. Experience teaches that saints are always clear-sighted in spiritual matters, because they have been divinely enlightened. Two examples come to mind: St. Teresa of Avila and St. Thérèse of Lisieux. Both saints had a profound grasp of deep theological truths because both were on fire with love for our Lord.

This brings up an interesting question: what is a theologian in the strict sense of the word? Is he exclusively a learned priest, one versed in ecclesiastical sciences, a doctor of theology? In other words, are "theologian" and "doctor" convertible terms?

No, not always, for there are certain theologians with a true and extensive knowledge of divine things who are not doctors in the academic sense of the word. Nevertheless they merit the title of "theologian" because they have a knowledge of God and His mysteries which sometimes has a depth far exceeding that of certain doctors.

Let us never forget that the supreme pinnacle which is God — His nature, His workings through grace, His ways and His plans — infinitely surpasses the power of all created intelligences. Certainly our faculties are indispensable instruments and they are a necessary starting point. Moreover, study is a natural need and for the priest is a grave duty binding in conscience. But we must never forget that the knowledge of God and divine things acquired by study is always restricted and limited.

When the theologian, then, desires to reach the inaccessible and unapproachable heights of God, he requires other means than talent, other lights than those acquired by mere study. He must also possess the powerful and divine enlightenment that comes from prayer. Only when he really knows how to pray, as well as and better than he knows how to study, will heaven descend toward him and unfold itself before him; then the man of God and of prayer will ascend to heights unknown to the genius; then the saint will *see* what the merely wise and learned will never see nor understand.

* * * * *

He, then, who wishes to be a true theologian in the spiritual sense of the word — and all priests should aspire to possess this beautiful title — must necessarily aim at becoming, through humility and prayer, "one who sees," a *videns*, like Moses on the mountain.

It can never be sufficiently emphasized or repeated too often (especially to seminarians) that to know, to penetrate the mysteries of God, a theologian must be not only a learned man, but in a far greater measure a man of deep interior life, a man of God; not a mere searcher of libraries but a man deeply in love with the tabernacle, a friend, and an intimate friend, of the only real Master, Jesus Christ.

Who really knows our Lord as much as He can be known here below? Only the friend to whom Christ manifests Himself; only he to whom, in the intimacy of prayer, He reveals secrets which He does not make known to the learned ones of this world.

What astonishing things are known to the friends of Jesus, even by those who have never studied! Thomas Aquinas reached the skies by his prodigious talents; but *Saint* Thomas went far beyond. This often happens to the humble who have no opportunity to read or study like Thomas, but who like him have prayed and meditated. "*. . .you have revealed to the merest children*" (Matt. 11:25).

Here is a striking example I have often related and one that caused the late Cardinal Billot to say when he heard it, "This should be written in letters of gold as a lesson in theology for seminarians and priests." Struck by the enlightened comments made by a peasant at Lourdes on one of my sermons on the Sacred Heart of Jesus, the King and Friend of Christian families, I invited him to come to my hotel. My idea was to listen to him at my ease and take notes on his simple but doctrinal commentaries. He came punctually and at my request began to comment again on the subject of my sermon. I was so amazed at the wisdom and eloquence of this peasant that I forgot even to take notes of his words, save for a few thoughts here and there.

However, I made up my mind I was not going to lose the lesson so providentially given to me. So I begged him to send me all he was saying in several letters, writing them if he wished in pencil. For a while he was silent, but when I insisted, he burst out laughing, saying, "But I do not know how to read or write."

Taken off guard, I exclaimed, "Then who has taught you all this?"

Here is the marvelous answer he gave me, spoken in grave tones, but quite simply: "As a priest you say Mass daily, as a Christian I receive Holy Communion daily. Therefore we both have the same Master. It is He who has taught me all I know."

I remained silent with astonishment. Thinking I had not understood, he explained himself by a comparison of extraordinary doctrinal simplicity:

"Father, suppose this table were an altar. You are there holding in your hands Jesus, the true Sun. Close to you and to Him am I, about to receive Communion. Between us, Jesus, the Sun. If I see Him and you do not, it is not the fault of the Sun, but of your eyes!"

Is this not admirable? Many masters and doctors do not know what this theologian — taught from the tabernacle — knew.

Certainly we need theologians everywhere — men with the theological knowledge willed by God and demanded by the Church, but also with souls aflame and hearts on fire like that of the peasant of Lourdes. Science without a deep interior life, book-theology without love of God and priestly holiness — *scientia sine caritate* — is a weak electric light that leaves vast spaces in total darkness.

Once more, studies are necessary both in and out of the seminary — for this is a duty binding in conscience. But to believe more in study than in the divine Master in the tabernacle is a grave and dangerous error, both for seminarian and for priest.

Never forget that all treatises of theology are merely prefaces to the living Book — Jesus Christ Himself! Try to acquire both "light and heat"; develop the light through the flame; love without measure, and the Lord will treat you as an intimate friend; He will manifest Himself to you as He promised: "He who loves Me will win My Father's love, and I too will love him, and will reveal Myself to him." Then, and only then, will He teach you the things He has heard from His Father, *"I have made known to you all that I heard from my Father"* (John 15:15).

"Come after Me," says our Lord. "I am the Light of the world and he who follows Me does not walk in darkness."

* * * * *

From what has been said already another important lesson can be drawn. There is not only the mystery of God but also that of souls. You are priests for them. This brings us face to face with a great mystery which engrossed all the saints and should be of paramount concern to us.

By the fact of our office as priests, we are directors and advisors, whose words, example and teaching will have eternal consequences. It has been well said, "Priests are the mouth of God, the spoken word of the invisible Word." This adds an overwhelming weight to our responsibility if we do not live up to it. And the responsibility is all the greater inasmuch as the faithful are obliged to consult us, to obey and let themselves be guided by us.

To direct souls inside of and outside of the confessional, to trace out their path, to show them their duty, to help them make decisions with consequences in time and eternity — all this is a great privilege, but also a great responsibility.

It is far from sufficient, then, that the priest be a good administrator, a good business man. God, the Church, souls, expect more from him than this. He is expected to be the father of the souls confided to him, the dispenser of the sacraments, the guide and counsellor of his people; the shepherd who knows his sheep by name. He is not only the motor which raises the plane, but also the pilot who directs its course.

Here we may ask: who is the priest who is a true counsellor and director of souls, full of wisdom, prudence, and zeal, with the tact of a father, the clear-sightedness of a doctor, the devotedness of a true apostle? This chosen and privileged priest is none other than the friend of Jesus who has already given him the key to His Heart as a reward for his piety. With this same key he can unlock the tabernacle-door of the heart of man, for one and the same key fits the Heart of Jesus and souls!

This is the way that doctors of the Church, such as St. Francis de Sales, and simple priests like the Curé of Ars, learned to penetrate the depths of the human conscience. Certainly they consulted treatises on moral theology; but more often they consulted the Master. He is the only one who can enlighten the priest in the solution of certain cases which no book can foresee.

Be quite convinced that the "paternity of souls," even more than that of nature, is a mystery and also a gift which can come only from on high. The solution of this problem presupposes a priestly soul moulded by grace and by the twofold light of study and a deep interior life. Both are necessary in order to avoid mistakes and blunders, the consequences of which may be fatal and irreparable. *"It is these you should have practiced, without neglecting the others"* (Matt. 23:23).

The act of guiding souls is a divine work and extremely difficult; only priests of much prayer, real men of God, can excel in it. To cooperate with Him in His plan of redemption, God in His wisdom never makes use of a merely "good, honest priest" who does his work mechanically, even though he be a great intellectual.

If you really want to be doctors in this double science of knowing God and of being able to penetrate into the secrets of souls, often meditate before the tabernacle on this wonderful assertion of St. Thomas Aquinas: "When I desire to see clearly and to sound the depths of some supernatural mystery, I plunge my mind, my head and my heart into the tabernacle."

To solve the problem of really knowing our Lord and souls, go often to the tabernacle to speak heart to heart with the Heart of the Master.

Magister adest et vocat te.

15. "Bethany of the Sacred Heart"

I have been requested to give a doctrinal definition of the work of the Enthronement of the Sacred Heart in the home, which I have been preaching for so many years. I acquiesce most willingly to this request. With the simplicity which for many years has been my sole apostolic eloquence, I shall write down, in the form of a fraternal heart-to-heart talk, just what I mean by the Enthronement, and exactly what is its doctrinal basis. The Breath of the Holy Spirit will do the rest! May the adorable Paraclete, who is Light and Fire, pour down upon these lines a veritable Pentecost, which will be at once a "vision" and a "love!" To see clearly and to love much — in these consist the classical gifts which make an apostle. May the loving Queen of Apostles and of the Cenacle take part in this modest work — for such is her right — so that its supernatural success may be as perfect as possible!

My exposition will be made up of three chapters: I. The Doctrine of the Sacred Heart of Jesus; II. The Revelation at Paray-le-Monial; III. The Enthronement of the Sacred Heart in the Home (as it has been approved and blessed by Rome). May the Well-Beloved be in my heart, and in the hearts of those who will read these lines, *ut adveniat Regnum Regis amoris!* ("That the kingdom of the King of Love may come!")

    I. THE DOCTRINE OF THE SACRED HEART OF JESUS.

Let me make it clear at the outset that I am writing for all friends of the Sacred Heart, but especially for priests, to whom I address myself with mingled feelings of respect and priestly tenderness.

Necessarily we begin with some fundamental principles. For we must be on our guard against a deformation of our work, brought about by the very fact of its development. The evil of "elephantiasis" in Catholic activities is much more common than one thinks. The body — that is to say, the organism — very often over-develops to the detriment of the soul, the spirit. Yet, on the other hand, development is but a law of nature and of grace. As a matter of fact, every living thing in nature and in the Church must grow and evolve, or wither and die.

The same holds true of virtue and sanctity, of intellectual and moral qualities, and likewise of Catholic activities. Time was when these were but grains of mustard seed in the hands of the Sower, then growing plants, and finally great trees sheltering the birds of the air. But in their very growth there is always some danger.

This is exactly the case with the Enthronement. In 1908 in Valparaiso, Chile, it was but a grain of mustard seed; today it is, thanks be to God, a great tree whose branches cover the entire earth, and whose fruits delight the friends of the King of Love and the very angels in heaven. But, needless to say, if the roots and sap are always the same, the tree of today has characteristics, or better, has developed a spiritual beauty and a supernatural fecundity which were present only potentially when the seedling was transplanted from the nursery of Paray-le-Monial to the garden of Valparaiso. And this is as it should be, for it is a perfectly normal phenomenon.

Let me explain. If those who listen to me today in Canada had heard me in 1908, they would easily remark that the style, or rather, the tone of the preacher has considerably changed, even though the dominant theme of his preaching is the same. Today there is less "color" and "music" in the presentation of his theme; for he lays greater stress on its doctrinal aspect, which he expounds, not with less sincerity, but with a stronger and more apostolic conviction.

No one should be surprised if I say that I have learned to preach by preaching, according to the axiom: "Fabricando fit faber." "One learns how to build by building." In the measure that I advanced, I understood more clearly that in the apostolate of the Social Reign of the Heart of Jesus it was necessary to place on the same footing, in perfect doctrinal harmony, the sublime teaching of St. Paul on charity and the revelations of the Sacred Heart at Paray-le-Monial. If the *liturgical cult* of the Sacred Heart was cradled in the chapel of Paray-le-Monial, the wonderful *doctrine* of the Sacred Heart stems from Bethlehem and Gethsemane, from Calvary and the Cenacle, from the inspired writings of St. John and St. Paul.

* * * * *

Yes, in our preaching we must inseparably unite St. Paul's theology of charity to devotion to the Sacred Heart, which the Church has so clearly approved and so strongly encouraged. Think of it — what a sublime and glorious hymn could be modeled on the sacred text: "The love of Christ impels us. . .love is the fulfilling of the law." The celestial melody of this would be: "Behold this Heart which has loved men so much. . . . I will reign through My Heart!" Our preaching will be one hundred per cent more effective, if we unite the statements of St. Paul and St. Margaret Mary — that is to say, the Pauline thesis on love and the authentic doctrine of St. Margaret Mary, presented to us by Holy Mother Church, as she blessed the devotion to the Sacred Heart.

When one has meditated on and appreciated the sublime passage which begins: "If I speak with the tongues of men and angels, but have not charity, I am nothing," then and then only will the "sitio" and the complaints, the requests and the promises of the King of Love, speaking to the Church through St. Margaret Mary, have an irresistible power and a sovereign claim on our souls.

The triumphant eloquence of a true apostle comes from the truth of the doctrine which he expounds. We shall conquer souls if, in the apostolate of the Enthronement and in all that concerns the Sacred Heart, we begin with what I like to call "the altar stone" — namely, the Gospel and St. Paul. Only afterwards do we place on this magnificent altar the "candles and flowers" (practices of devotion) asked for by St. Margaret Mary in honor of the Sacred Heart.

* * * * *

Is it not true that very often our apostolate is reduced too much to the level of a simple devotion, and that we do not insist enough on that doctrinal substance underlying this incomparable devotion? If the cause of the Sacred Heart is not yet completely won, especially among the clergy, is this not due partly to an imperfect presentation of the subject, or at least to one that is not sufficiently doctrinal?

The Enthronement helps to bring out the depths of the relationship of ideal and doctrine between the great Apostle to the Gentiles and the Messenger of Paray-le-Monial — between St. Paul saying: "He loved me and delivered Himself for me. He who loves, has fulfilled the Law," and the revelations of the requests and complaints of the Heart of Jesus, but also His promises that He, the King of Love, will reign by the power of His Heart, despite Satan and his agents!

To grasp more clearly the inseparable doctrinal bond between *doctrine* and *devotion*, let us make a simple comparison. The Hail Mary, and hence the Rosary and the entire Marian cult of Lourdes and Fatima, are based on the Mystery of the Annunciation or, more properly, on the dogma of the Divine Maternity of Mary. For we must never forget that in the first place comes "Marian theology," on which is constructed, as a Catholic monument of the first rank, "Marian devotion."

Our friends and collaborators should be made to understand clearly that every devotion, in the strict sense of the word, *always presupposes a dogma;* a devotion, to be truly Catholic, must be thoroughly dogmatic.

* * * * *

Now, among the numerous and very beautiful devotions approved by the Church there is certainly not one more "dogmatic," more "evangelical," than devotion to the Sacred Heart of Jesus. For it embraces in an enlightening and solid manner the three great chapters which contain the "Credo" of our Catholic Faith, namely: a.) the mystery of love, the Incarnation; b.) the mystery of love which is the "folly of the cross"; and c.) the gift of love, *par excellence*, the Eucharist — sacrifice and sacrament.

Enlightened by this fundamental doctrine, we shall grasp more readily both the beauty and the significance of the requests concerning the Feast of the Sacred Heart, the celebration of the First Fridays in a spirit of eucharistic and reparative love; the Holy Hour, vigil of penance and reparation; and finally the consecration to the Sacred Heart (that is, to His Love) of all that is beautiful and vital in the Church, honoring at the same time in an explicit manner the image of this adorable Heart, the maternal symbol of His infinitely merciful love. The word "heart" is a symbolic, figurative term in both human and divine language. Therefore, when the Savior says: "Behold this Heart which has loved men so much," this is equivalent to saying: "Contemplate in My Heart the love I have for you . . . and in exchange for this Heart, for My love, give Me your love, your heart."

The great Cardinal Pie expressed this idea magnificently when he said: "The whole Christ, from His Head crowned with thorns through love, to His Feet pierced through love, is nothing but an infinite Heart, who through His wounds offers naught but love, and claims nothing but love in return."

As a final comparison to clarify the foundation of this

doctrinal alliance between the Gospel, St. Paul, and Paray-le-Monial, let us suppose that the thesis, *"Caritas Christi urget nos,"* were a masterpiece of sacred painting. The frame best suited to display this painting would be the revelations of Paray-le-Monial. Again, if this sublime thesis *"Dilexit me et tradidit semetipsum pro me"* were (let us say) a Mass, the practical and sacred formula for celebrating this Mass would be, again, devotion to the Sacred Heart, the external form of worship as proposed by St. Margaret Mary and approved by the Church.

* * * * *

What did Jesus the King say at Paray? Fundamentally, He repeated what He had already preached by His tears and His miracles, in the crib, on Calvary, and in the Cenacle. "Behold this Heart which has loved you so much, and which has performed these marvels in order to make Itself loved. I desire to conquer and possess you by the power of My love."

To close this section, I propose to make two statements, both striking and doctrinal. The first is: "Unum est credere, aliud est amare." ("It is one thing to believe, quite another to love.") An act of faith, the submission of the mind to a revealed truth or to a mystery, is not of itself an act of charity, the gift of self, which is called love. As a matter of fact, we can believe (and St. Paul even speaks of faith that can move mountains), but if we do not live our faith by love, then that faith merely makes us more responsible. Oh, yes, one can believe without loving, but one cannot love without believing! A true Christian is he who believes with a great faith, but who also loves what he believes with an even greater love. The perfection of faith, of hope, and all the virtues is charity, or love!

It follows that *to preach faith is only half of the Gospel;* therefore, let us preach love which perfects and vivifies faith. Note well that Jesus complains of a lack of love! Does that mean that the other virtues are to be found in abundance? Not at all! On the contrary, when love, the queen and source of virtues, is lacking, the rest will be lacking too.

Let us who are preaching the Heart of Jesus be apostles of love! Love is certainly not a sickly feeling, still less an effeminate sentimentality, but the *total gift of self*, the ability and the grace to give oneself to Him who out of love has delivered Himself for us! The God of Love whom we adore and preach wants to be loved absolutely!

* * * * *

As a second and final observation on this admirable doctrine of love, I would speak here of three ineffable gifts which the love of the Heart of Jesus has presented to His Church.

The *very first gift* is the knowledge and love of His Father. "Prompted by divine instruction, we make bold to say, *Our Father.*" Here we have basically the wonderful novelty of the Gospel: "God, our Father; we, His adopted children!" It took nothing less than the Incarnate Word to reveal to us this mystery of divine love, supreme gift of a supreme love. And ever since that revelation we call the Man-God our eldest Brother; His Father is our Father, and His Mother is our Mother!

The *second gift* is Himself. He gives Himself to us forever. He is our Treasure, our Good! And this gift is irrevocable; the Eucharist fixes His abode among us in this land of exile; "Until the consummation of the world."

The *third gift*, worthy of the adorable Giver, is *Pentecost.* "It is expedient for you that I depart. For if I do not go, the Advocate will not come to you, but if I go, I will send him to you" (John 16:7). The Holy Spirit did come, and on Calvary the Church was born.

Truly, since the love of Jesus bestowed these three wonderful gifts upon us, we can almost say that omnipotence has exhausted itself. And as He promised, when we love Him who is Love Incarnate, the three Divine Persons take up their abode in us, and we become living monstrances of the most august Trinity. We who preach the Enthronement should break this alabaster vase so that every home of the Sacred Heart may be thoroughly filled with the odor of the thrice-holy oil of this sublime doctrine.

Once more, let us proclaim in season and out of season that the great doctors of this divine theology of love are Paul and John the Evangelist, Bonaventure and Bernard, Thomas Aquinas and Francis de Sales, St. John Eudes. Yes, long before the beautiful devotion to the Sacred Heart was revealed through St. Margaret Mary, these spiritual giants were already the great apostles of the Heart of Jesus.

If we preach in this way, we shall transform the marvelous little Chapel of Paray-le-Monial into a truly Catholic sanctuary! This was the thought of Leo XIII when he said: "The greatest private revelation was the one made at Paray-le-Monial. After Calvary, its altar is the most sacred, and around it gravitates the thought and love of the Church."

"I am a King," were the words of Jesus before Pilate, and St. Paul declares: "For He must reign." But before the ecstatic eyes of St. Margaret Mary, He assures us that He longs to reign and that He will reign through His Heart! It is for this reason the Church forbids the crowning of the image of the Sacred Heart: Jesus is King by nature, and also by right of conquest through the holy cross of redemption.

II. THE REVELATIONS TO ST. MARGARET MARY AT PARAY-LE-MONIAL

Let us enter, on bended knee, this new Gethsemane, which still echoes with the sad complaints and stirring requests of the King of Love. Its history is well-known; therefore, I shall merely recall briefly the statements of the Savior to His confidante and messenger.

Jesus repeats over and over that He thirsts for love. But He complains bitterly of so-called friends, of mediocre friends who wound His Heart, because they do not truly love Him. The King of Love is indeed a beggar for love! He desires to reign, He must reign, because He is a King; but he wills to reign, not by destroying, but by converting and pardoning. But above all, consecrated souls must love Him with a perfect love! Priests and religious, the appeal and perhaps the reproach are especially for us! Note well, the greatest promise concerns us: "I will sanctify My friends by a special grace." Happy those who understand that the Good Master desires to perpetuate the succession of John, the beloved disciple. Yes, He wants intimate friends — "Johns," of whom He wants to make "Pauls," apostles of fire.

For our own sake let us stress this idea. Jesus desires and demands of us, His consecrated friends, a love unto sanctity. To His fervent and faithful friends He promises an extraordinary grace, a sort of charism, that of converting and softening the most hardened hearts. But let us never forget, the apostle most powerful in the work of salvation is always the intimate friend who, having won the Heart of Jesus, dispenses His treasures for His glory and the salvation of souls.

* * * * *

Naturally this leads us to the pleasant but important duty of reparation, characteristic of devotion to the Sacred Heart. A love which is thrust aside, forgotten, and outraged, demands from friends a kind of compensation, which, having appeased His justice, obtains an outpouring of mercy. Because He is truly a just God, He finds Himself obliged to punish and chastise: for He is as much Justice as Love. But as far as we, poor exiles, are concerned, one would say He is more a "divine pity," more a dispenser of mercy, than of rigorous and vengeful justice.

Still, in order to restore the balance upset by sin, He urges us to make reparation, to offer Him a penitent love, so that, His justice appeased, He may exercise His mercy. For this purpose, He Himself places the purchase price in our hands. Thus, He asks that the First Friday be consecrated to Him in a special way as a homage of eucharistic and reparative love. As a recompense for this offering of love, He gives special graces. Finally, He asks St. Margaret Mary to rise at night to watch with Him, to console Him even better than the angel at Gethsemane. And so He institutes the Holy Hour which from that time on has played such a great part in the extension of the reign of the Sacred Heart.

* * * * *

But, let it be well noted, just as the greatest revelation took place during the exposition of the Blessed Sacrament on December 27, the feast of St. John, so also the entire message of Paray is eminently *Eucharistic*. By this I mean that, in the history of the revelations of the Heart of Jesus, everything stems from the Eucharist, and everything without exception returns to the Eucharist.

As will soon be pointed out, in this eucharistic love we must maintain the scale of doctrinal values which places before everything else the eucharistic sacrifice, Holy Mass, as the foundation and source of all eucharistic piety. After that comes Holy Communion, the tabernacle, and the monstrance for adoration and other practices of devotion.

The great feast of the Sacred Heart is a splendid summary of all the requests, and it should become through our efforts a striking triumph for the King of Love. Regarding this feast, let us remember that it is the Savior Himself who selected and fixed the day of its celebration. As much as possible, let us keep to this day and not transfer this marvelous feast to a Sunday, for very special graces are attached to it. Encourage the families of the Sacred Heart to make it a true family feast so that the doctrine and the devotion of the Heart of Jesus may become a sacred tradition in the home, one to be handed down, as are family traits, from generation to generation.

Finally, Jesus is so determined to make us understand His desire to be ardently loved, that He demands a special homage for the very symbol of His love to which He deigns to attach special blessings.

The golden key to this chapter on Paray is a moving parallel between Margaret Mary and Thérèse of Lisieux — two great saints, truly twins because of their intimate vocation, although quite different in their style and their mission, yet two conquering, triumphant messengers of the King of Love, who begs for love. The two would seem to be born in the wound of the Sacred Heart. Indeed, a flame has been enkindled wherever the message of St. Margaret Mary has penetrated, and the same is true of Thérèse, wherever her autobiography has made her known.

What a supernatural affinity, despite some very great differences, between the victim of Paray and that of Lisieux, both of them holocausts of love, both apostles of love and mercy! Two statements sum up the ideal of the two providential missionaries of love.

"My vocation is to love," says St. Thérèse. "No, I cannot take any rest until the end of the world . . . then I shall be able to rejoice because the number of the elect will be complete!"

"To love Him unto folly," says St. Margaret Mary, "and to make Him greatly loved, that is enough for me."

May they be our guiding stars!

III. THE ENTHRONEMENT OF THE SACRED HEART IN THE HOME.

As founder of this work, I have been asked to give a definition which corresponds exactly to its ideal and spirit. *In nomine Domini*, I shall do my best.

Is the Enthronement nothing more than the image installed in the place of honor? No; there is more to it than that! Is it perhaps but a beautiful and simple consecration of the family to the Sacred Heart? The consecration is included indeed, but there is much more than that!

What then? There is a marvelous statement made by Jesus to St. Margaret Mary which I give as a synthesis of our crusade, at least as far as its supreme ideal is concerned: *"I will reign through My Heart and I promise to reign!"* The Enthronement is the apostolate which is trying to make this divine affirmation something lived in the home, the social cell. That is why the idea of *royalty* expressed by the term "Enthronement" is not just an arbitrary title given to our work, and that is also the reason that I have continued to use it, despite criticisms of all kinds, for in itself it constitutes an entire program of action.

Here is another definition, more technical in content: the Enthronement is the homage of adoration, of social reparation, and of fervent love, which the family, as the social cell, offers to the Heart of Jesus considered as King of Society. In this sense, which is strictly doctrinal, the Enthronement is not merely a beautiful but simple consecration; it is the homage of *adoration*, made in a spirit of love and reparation for the *modern social apostasy*. In other words, it is the *Ave Rex*, (Hail, King) the "We want this Man to rule over us," of the Family, the "nation in miniature."

Now, how bring about in daily family life the practical application of this doctrine of the divine rule of Jesus? By carrying out in the home, not one or another of the requests made at Paray, but indeed *every one of them*. One of these requests refers to the honor to be given to the image of the Sacred Heart. This image is only a symbol, a reminder, of the presence in the home of a living King, recognized as such in everyday life. But since it is the King of Love who is enthroned, it goes without saying that it is the entire doctrine of St. Paul on love which is presented to the family as an ideal, as it is likewise the integral devotion of Paray-le-Monial that we propose to the family as its very heart and soul. Thus the family becomes the living throne of a King whose sovereign dominion is accepted with as much faith as love.

The well-beloved King of Love is at the same time the great Friend of His friends at Bethany: "You are my friends." And He is even more a King among His own, precisely because He is a true Friend, loved wholeheartedly. Thus, a great intimacy should be established between this King and His friends, an intimacy which is the outpouring of hearts filled with confidence like those of Lazarus, Martha, and Mary, into the ever-faithful loving Heart of their Divine Friend. And this friendship must result in an intimate sharing of the daily life of the family with Jesus, and consequently of Jesus with the family: "Stay with us" (Luke 24:29).

The family of the Sacred Heart must never take its pleasures or sorrows alone; Jesus, the Friend, always has His part, and the very first, at that, in the sorrowful and joyous happenings of parents and children. For His Heart is the very center of this happy family. Naturally, this means that on certain outstanding family celebrations and cherished anniversaries, on First Fridays, the family should gather at the feet of the royal Friend, and renew its offering of total love to the Heart of Jesus. There you have Jesus Christ become a God-Emmanuel in the Christian home.

But all of this necessarily presupposes a great eucharistic fervor. Consequently, the home must become, little by little, a veritable *sanctuary*. Therefore, *daily Mass and Communion must become for the family a law of love, and pressing necessity, in truth its daily Bread!*

\)   * * * * *

This is the proper place to emphasize a principle which is not always understood or practiced in pious circles: namely, that in eucharistic love the Holy Sacrifice of the Mass must always occupy the first place. Alas, for many good Christians the Eucharist consists merely of Holy Communion. They do not come to Mass for the purpose of adoring, praising and blessing the Most Holy Trinity, *"Through Him, with Him, in Him,"* but only in order to receive Holy Communion. For too many Holy Mass is, after all, but the liturgical key which opens the tabernacle door. The official praise given to God by the Church through the Holy Sacrifice of the Mass is very often entirely overlooked.

Let us do our best to re-establish the scale of spiritual values in a manner of such transcendent importance. Sacrifice and sacrament must remain inseparable, but the Sacred Fountain, without which there is neither Communion rail, nor tabernacle, nor monstrance, is the Holy Sacrifice: "Inexhaustible fountain of life." A great theologian has well said: "He who does not appreciate Holy Mass will never be a eucharistic soul; daily Communion itself will be a matter of routine and without fruit if the chalice is not recognized as the fountain." Yes, families of the Sacred Heart should love Holy Mass with their whole heart and soul.

* * * * *

In order to increase the flame of charity, let us light that lamp of penitent and reparative love, *nocturnal adoration in the home.* This means that we should try to organize, even though it be with groups of elite families, a eucharistic vigil, a perpetual Holy Hour. Here again we have a Bethany turned into a sanctuary, a tabernacle.

Nocturnal adoration has had a success which has surprised even the most optimistic, including myself. But its success in the supernatural order has been everywhere a spiritual renovation, a rebirth of eucharistic fervor — and I might add, a source of remarkable conversions! It is in itself a remarkable powerhouse of grace, for it comprises the three vital elements of Christian life, prayer, expiation, and love. Therefore you, who are apostles, hold fast to this apostolate with all your hearts, but see to it that *you yourselves are the very first adorers in spirit and in truth!* With this supernatural method of apostolate, then, make the Enthronement a work of social salvation! In it find the means of the sanctification of friends, and for the conversion of so many who are lukewarm and for sinners, found in great numbers even in the best families.

Our work has always had its special characteristic;

indeed, it has been "canonized" by heaven. It has harvested for the granaries of the Father a great number of publicans who have been mortally ill. It possesses the secret of conversion and spiritual resurrection. But since I am speaking to apostles, I allow myself an obervation: if the marvel of grace which is the Holy Mass does not succeed in sanctifying all who offer it (and this because of our own fault), the Enthronement, *ex opere operato*, cannot be expected to do more! Thus, it is absolutely necessary that we, the apostles, make up our minds to live to the full the law of charity and the spirit of love, which we preach to families. This is what I call the *sincerity* of our preaching.

The King will give in superabundance whatever He has promised, but only on condition that we be, like Margaret Mary, extremely docile instruments, ready to live and to preach His love.

* * * * *

At this point, I must not omit certain counsels of extreme importance for the progress of our work. I mean to say that, not satisfied with contributing to the divine victory with all the fire of our faith and our enthusiasm, we must also multiply around us apostles of the social reign of the Heart of Jesus.

Religious communities, be they devoted to prayer and penance or consecrated to the work of education, will become an incomparable army if they are truly won to this cause.

Wonderful conquests have been made, due to the zeal of our junior apostles, members of the League of St. Tarcisius. Wherever Sisters have wholeheartedly tried to stimulate their students by enkindling the flame of zeal, they have witnessed the power which the childlike hearts wield over the Heart of Jesus. Piety without zeal is nothing but a flash without an aftermath; but piety with zeal is a God-given blessed fire, a fire which radiates, and which endures. There is no doubt that the greatest profit from this apostolate comes to the communities, for they bring down upon themselves the blessings promised by the Heart of Jesus. But we must not forget that there is also a great blessing for the spiritual welfare and the perseverance of the student-apostles. Let us train them as early as possible in the duty of the apostolate, a duty which is one of solid piety of true love.

Let us also utilize the communities engaged in charitable works, and ask them to contribute their sacrifices and their sufferings to the extension of the reign of the Sacred Heart. I make a suggestion here which already has had excellent results: that the Sisters and nurses in hospitals should continue to be enrolled in nocturnal adoration. How powerful it is to have thousands of nurses making their nocturnal adoration beside the bed of the sick and dying, and thus proving their solicitude for the agonizing and crucified King, as well as for their suffering charges! For this great army of charitable workers, and their unfortunate charges, the apostolate of suffering will become a marvelous supernatural solace, and at the same time will contribute most efficaciously to the success of our apostolate. For to suffer with love as an apostle means that one is already preaching with an eloquence which is always fruitful.

And now to close in a serious vein, the present situation of society and of the world is extremely grave. Yet, we must have confidence in Him who has conquered the world! I myself heard the great Pius XI solemnly declare *"Humanity is living in its darkest hour since the deluge. But the Church has a great hope of salvation, for we are living to the full the hour of the Sacred Heart."* "I will reign despite Satan and his agents," was the explicit statement of the King, but He added that He would reign through His Heart! And the rock on which we must construct the Christian fortress is, and will always remain, the home, under attack today with a diabolical hatred. It is true that the tempest of hate, which is concentrating on the family, is fear-inspiring. Nevertheless, we have cause to rejoice, for we have His marvelous promises. "Help will fail you," said the King to St. Margaret Mary, "only when I shall be lacking in power."

Thus, if the King of Love is with us, who shall stand against Him, and against us?

In conclusion, I wish to stress very strongly the importance and timeliness of the Enthronement. We have placed it in the ranks of a true crusade, and indeed it merits this title in the strict meaning of the word. For what could be greater as an enterprise of social salvation than the work of saving the Christian fortress — the home, where the Sacred Heart reigns as King, and where He is loved as an adorable Friend? What is more powerful than a home which is a tabernacle of prayer, a tabernacle of eucharistic fervor, and a sanctuary of Christian penance? There you have in spirit and in truth the authentic Bethany of the Heart of Jesus.

When the Enthronement merited the blessing and even the praise of St. Pius X, Benedict XV, Pius XI, and Pius XII, it was precisely because they considered it as a work of Christian restoration, and an apostolic organism of the highest value. If, in this great struggle, the Church protects us, and encourages us in such a maternal and wholehearted way, certainly we may be permitted to say that God is with us. "Let us also go, that we may die with Him! For He must reign!"

16. To the King of Love Through the Queen of Hearts

This allocution was delivered by Father Mateo on September 10, 1921, during, a Marian Congress at Brussels. The occasion was a gathering of the Association of Priests of Mary. His Eminence Cardinal Mercier presided at the meeting which was attended by well-known ecclesiastics including the Superior General of the Company of Mary and of the Congregation of Wisdom. Later, this discourse was published with an introduction by Cardinal Mercier. In it the great Cardinal said in part:

"In this allocution the fervent apostle of the Sacred Heart seems to wish to synthesize these great devotions: *to live a life of union with Jesus* in order to enter more profoundly into the secrets of love contained in the Immaculate and Sorrowful Heart of Mary; *to live a life of union with Mary* in order to go through her to Jesus; to become a slave of the Queen of Love as 'the King-Jesus despoiled Himself in her womb, becoming her own, her child and her captive nine months before Bethlehem and for thirty years at Nazareth;' and to do this 'not out of fear of Jesus but because I am certain that by going to Him through Mary I love and please Him more; I correspond with His providential designs thereby increasing a hundred times over the value of my gift.'

"Worthy of our meditations are these words of the

servant of Mary, St. Louis Marie de Montfort: 'Many do not reach the fullness of the age of Christ because Mary is not sufficiently formed in them.'

"My dear brother priests, all of us long to reach the fullness of the age of Christ; let us then allow Mary to perfect in us her work as our Mother. Listen to the voice of her dying Jesus: *"Woman, there is your son"* (John 19:26).

* * * * *

Allow me to praise you, O Holy Virgin!
The Most beautiful homage that can be offered to Mary is a diadem, the jewels of which are priests of Mary.

Although this crown is in itself a priceless gift — *Sacerdos al Christus* (The priest is another Christ) — still its value can and should be enhanced by sacerdotal sancity and to such a degree that every priest may dare to say in all truth, *Ego Ipse Jesus* (I am Jesus Himself).

Let me explain. On Easter morning, Jesus, glorious and transfigured, presented Himself to Mary. Her ecstasy of sorrow was suddenly transformed into one of jubilant happiness. Jesus, dead to the life of the body, had found in the tomb a new and glorious life.

Now He stands before Mary and tells her: "Mother change your mourning and your tears into joy: *Ego Ipse Jesus.* I am your son. Do you not recognize Me? Once more you have found your Jesus."

That the Queen of Mercy may recognize *her Jesus* in each of us, more and more she must find in our priestly souls the elements which constitute the well-formed priest:

God acting through us; tremendous power: *Alter Christus.*

God acting in us; element of priestly holiness: *Ego Ipse Jesus."*

Power and holiness — a sublime dignity together with superhuman powers grafted onto a nature of average supernatural life, of ordinary virtue. A lack of balance here could be dangerous. Who is going to re-establish the proper equilibrium? Mary!

156

Sacerdotal powers are inherent in the Sacrament of Holy Orders. Holiness depends upon us in union with Mary. Thus it is up to us to establish a perfect balance in our priestly life by our fidelity to grace.

We need saintly priests and we need them urgently, for all signs point to the coming of a terrible crisis. Yet this crisis could result in another Pentecost, provided God receives the cooperation of *holy* priests. But why are there not enough of them? St. Louis Marie de Montfort answers: "Many do not reach the fullness of the age of Christ because Mary is not sufficiently formed in them. . . . He who wishes to have the fruit of life, Jesus Christ, must have the tree of life, which is Mary." She is the safest, the shortest and the most beautiful way: *"I will show you a still more excellent way"* (I Cor. 12:31).

Once again, see how the Holy Spirit, with the cooperation of Mary, creates this new Jesus, the priest. The Holy Spirit in union with Mary bestows upon him his external powers through the Sacrament of Orders, making him, as it were, the arm of God; the virginal and maternal fecundity of Mary, under the influence of the Holy Spirit, causes his interior virtues to bear fruit, forms in him the heart of God and produces the *saint!* "Know that this Mother of Divine Love possesses the secret of this wondrous union that My Heart now offers to every priest as a new grace of sanctification." Creatures — even good ones — can sometimes hinder our progress toward Christ. But Mary — never! Mary is the divine path that leads inevitably into the abyss of the Heart of Christ.

Inasmuch as she is *gratia plena*, Mary exercises a privileged mission with regard to priests. Ever since Calvary she is their Mother and Queen: *ecce filius tuus*. The priest is not "another son," but in a certain sense the same Jesus! It is to this mission of Mary in our regard that we can apply the beautiful and original commentary on her *Magnificat* of St. John Eudes, who interprets our Lady's words thus: "My soul develops the Lord," meaning that she causes Him to grow in glory, grace, and productivity in the person of His "other self" the saintly priest!

This is why Father Olier states, "we make more progress in sanctity in union with Mary than by all other means together." For this reason also I affirm: supposing Christ offered me one ordinary grace through Mary Mediatrix and a thousand others with her mediation; and supposing the King of Love left me free to choose, I would go to Mary, knowing that in her and in her alone I should find everything I need: *Qui me invenerit inveniet vitam* (Prov. 8:35).

Without further ado let us turn our attention to the dominant idea of this conference. In substance, all Christian perfection is based on the affirmation of this transcendent task: "to know and to love Jesus Christ." We are led by the Son, who is the way, to know the Father and to become cenacles of the Paraclete the Sanctifier, tabernacles in which the august Trinity are pleased to take up Their abode. "Now this is everlasting life, that they may know thee, the only true God, and him whom thou hast sent, Jesus Christ" (John 17:3). "No one comes to the Father but through me" (John 14:6). "If anyone love me, he will keep my word, and my Father will love him, and we will come to him and make our abode with him" (John 14:23).

Since we are now concerned expressly with Jesus and Mary let us consider for a few moments the *Son* and His *Mother*.

* * * * *

1. To know Jesus in the School of Mary.
2. To know Mary in the School of Jesus.

A fundamental preparation for becoming a priest of Mary is to know Jesus with the knowledge that comes to us through His Mother. Just as our Lord said, "No one knows the Son except the Father," so, though in a different degree, we may add, "Who after the Father has ever known Jesus as His mother knows Him?"

1. In the School of Mary

Let us follow the example of the apostles, especially that of St. John, the beloved disciple, and have recourse to the lessons taught by the mother of Jesus.

It was for them and for us that Mary "kept all these words in her heart," and it is to the peaceful and enlightening sanctuary of her Immaculate Heart that the Beloved invites those to whom He wishes to impart the secrets of His Heart (cf. Cant. 8:2).

To the priests of her Heart especially Mary wishes to make known two great and precious secrets of the King:

a.) The mystery of the hidden life of Jesus, which no one knew and understood as did His mother. Jesus showed Himself to her as to no one else. The interior life of a priest should be one of recollection, prayer, and a deep spirit of faith. And its indispensable basis must be this mystery of Nazareth — the interior life and action of Jesus known, pondered, and revealed by Mary.

b) The mystery of the hidden Passion of the Heart of Jesus, His secret Gethsemane both before and after the agony in the Garden. The knowledge of this mystery is absolutely necessary for the life of immolation and sacrifice a priest of Mary must lead, for like Jesus and Mary he is both *the offerer and victim.*

Priestly holiness presupposes a profound knowledge resulting from frequent meditation on these mysteries. And who holds the keys to them, except the Queen of Nazareth, the Mother of the Heart of Jesus?

The *Message of the Sacred Heart* to priests contains these words: "Many priests know the theory of union with Me, but how few there are, even among the most devoted of My friends, who know that I am there in the depths of their souls yearning to make them *one* with Me. . . . If only they would tear themselves away from material things and in solitude seek Me in the depths of their souls where I am, they would soon find Me, and what a life of union, light and love would be theirs! But let them go full of confidence to My mother who is also their mother. How she loves My priests! It is My sweet mother who urges

Me to open the treasures of My Heart to them all . . . but especially to My good priests.''

And *during* this exile show unto us the blessed fruit of thy womb, Jesus!

2. *In the School of Jesus*

St. Louis Marie de Montfort says that ignorance of Jesus comes especially from not knowing His mother. To remedy this, Mary's school and Mary the Teacher and Queen of Doctors must be more widely and better known. "Show us the Father," said the apostle; and we add "Show us also Thy mother. Reveal her to us, she who is Thy own glory!''

We know Mary more through Lourdes, Fatima and La Salette than through the personal teaching of her Son: that is why so often she is known so superficially.

All Mary's glory is within. Therefore only the King who has entered and lived in this sanctuary can teach us truly to know and love this unique virgin-mother who is all fair: *tota pulchra es Maria.*

Those who have studied in this school of prayer and personal friendship with the divine King have been without exception ardent lovers of Mary. Bernard, Bonaventure, Bernardine of Siena, Dominic, Alphonsus Liguori, Francis de Sales, John Eudes, Louis Marie de Montfort and other lovers of Mary have learned more about her while kneeling before the tabernacle than by reading books. In fact, one would say that an ardent love for Mary and an understanding of her Heart are gifts reserved for those who are loved by her Jesus as was St. John.

Do you not think that after Calvary, when the apostles gathered around Mary in the Cenacle, they must have begged her to share with them the treasures of her understanding and knowledge of our Lord? And Mary spoke to them, explaining many things not to be found in Scripture but which have been engraved in the heart of the Church. Likewise, before His Ascension, Jesus must have spoken about Mary to St. John and to His other disciples, as He gave them His last instructions. His words on Calvary were the official words of the Pontiff-King. Now He allowed His divine Heart to overflow into theirs.

This explains perhaps, at least in part, despite the mysterious silence of the evangelists, why theologians for twenty centuries have been able to draw unceasingly from the treasures of the Church the marvelous and inexhaustible riches of Marian doctrine.

From my own humble experience I have always found that eucharistic souls have a special facility for grasping in a most profound way the perfections of Mary and for entering intimately into the secrets of love of her Immaculate Heart. This proves that the way *par excellence* to know Mary thoroughly is friendship with her divine Son.

* * * * *

To love Jesus through Mary and as Mary with a pure, maternal, and personal love.

To love Mary as Jesus, even to the slavery of love.

The revelation of the Father through His Son, Jesus Christ, is perfected in charity. "Love therefore is the fulfillment of the Law" (Rom. 13:10). Let us love Jesus Christ who first loved us and who loved us *usque in finem.* Love Him as far as possible with the only love worthy of Him; love Jesus with the Heart and with the sentiments of Mary: *"I am the Mother of Fair Love."* "I am cold, hungry, thirsty! Tell My priests to warm Me with their love. This is what I ask of My priests whom I love dearly. Tell them how greatly I love them!" (*Message of the Sacred Heart to the Heart of the Priest.*)

You are familiar with these burning words of the *Message.* And the King adds, "It is My dear mother who urges Me to open the treasures of My Heart especially to My priests. It is this Mother of Divine Love who guards this secret."

Priestly love learned in and through the Heart of Mary should have three characteristics:

1. It should be *virginal* — that is to say, strong, intense, burning, unique, as Father Olier puts it. Jesus demands a *flame* of love, not a mere spark.

This virginal love must be also total and entire, concentrated exclusively on His divine person; a love ardent in prayer, generous when sacrifice is demanded.

In the *Message* our Lord tells us that to love with a virginal love means to gather together and to concentrate all one's affection on Him.

2. It should be *maternal*. Yes, maternal, especially at the altar. For at each Mass *Puer natus est nobis*. I would willingly renounce, O Mary, the ecstasy of Bethlehem and all the glory of an apostolic life in exchange for one flame of your love, that I might celebrate a single Mass in a manner worthy of you, My Queen and Mother!

Sacerdotal maternity consists in the total gift of self in exchange for the total gift the Father makes of His Son in the Holy Eucharist. "For God so loved the world that he gave his only-begotten Son" (John 3:16). The priest, in His turn, must love the Father and the Son by giving himself to them as Mary gave herself to the Father and to the Son when the Heart of Jesus first throbbed in the manger.

Oh, the Mass, mystery of love and grandeur! This is the time to prove ourselves true priests of Mary. A priest who understands the meaning of sacerdotal maternity, who knows how to give himself to Jesus through Mary, as Jesus gave Himself to the Father through Mary, is very close to being a saint.

In these critical times, why is there a lack of holy priests in pulpits, in confessionals and in Catholic Action? Because there are not enough holy priests at the altar. We who offer sacrifice must maternalize our love and celebrate Mass with the sentiments and tenderness of the Heart of Mary.

3. Priestly love must be warm and *personal*. This is the kind of love that draws us to the Heart of Jesus, guided, led, and encouraged by the Heart of Mary.

"If My priests only knew with what intense desire I long to unite Myself intimately to each one of them! But rare are those who attain the degree of union that My Heart has prepared for them on earth" (*Message*). Why? What is lacking? Faith — a strong faith in the love of Jesus — an intense confidence in the love of His Heart.

And it is here precisely, that I desire the intercession of the authentic mother of Jesus, who so often is presented to us as a shield of mercy against the just vengeance of a fear-inspiring Savior who actually is all love and mercy! How well the delicate shades of Mary's love were understood by the incomparable Louis Marie de Montfort! He writes: "We can and we should have recourse to the Mediatrix, to the mediation of Mary, not out of fear of Jesus, but because of the humility so fitting even in those who have a great love for the God of Love. *"When the kindness and love of God our Savior appeared, He saved us. . ."* (Titus, 3:4-7).

Jesus, all love, all merciful, calls to us, draws us to Himself; more than ever, in this age of His Sacred Heart, He repeats His consoling words, *"Fear not."* And if, to justify our fear, we allege our unworthiness to approach Him, He insists, *"Fear not. . .It is I."* — I am the God of Love, the Son of Mary, the Savior Jesus.

If Mary is kind, if Mary is tender, if Mary is merciful, it is because she shares in the kindness, the tenderness, the mercy of her divine Son.

Supposing I found one reason to fear to go through Mary, I would go directly to Jesus, for I must not and I will not fear Him, precisely because He is Jesus, the Savior. He satisfies divine justice as regards His Father, and He waits for me with the gift of His Heart to perfect not only the work of my salvation, but also of my sanctification through love.

Yet, following the example of my Redeemer, the God-Man who created Mary — Mediatrix for Himself and for us — I do not wish to go directly to Jesus. I prefer to go to Him through Mary. This I do, not out of fear of Jesus but to express a twofold love for Him, for I am certain that by going to Him through Mary I love and please Him more; and I correspond with His providential designs, thereby increasing and enhancing the mediation of Mary.

In this sense, I can say more freely and more joyously, "I love You, Jesus, because You are Jesus!" and in an accommodated sense, "I love you, Mary, because you are Mary!"

Thus the total offering of myself to the Queen of Love, the sweet Virgin Mary, is an expression of a deeper love, a much more filial love, a more selfless love: I give myself to her because she is the Mother of Jesus and my mother.

If to all these motives which are more than sufficient, I add, with St. Louis Marie de Montfort, that of humility, I increase the value of my sacrifice offered without reserve on the altar of the Immaculate Heart of Mary, my Queen, my Mediatrix and my Mother!

I adore God the Father with a peaceful, humble and salutary fear, but I go to Him full of confidence, carried in the blood-stained arms of my Savior. Overcome by confusion and love, I adore my Jesus and go trustingly to meet Him, my Savior, in the arms of Mary. For through her, *"I have found the Heart of a King, the Heart of a Brother, the Heart of a Friend, O most kind Jesus"* (St. Bernard).

If the phrase *"never enough about Mary"* is true of the external Marian apostolate exercised for her glory, how much more true it should be of the interior filial love we owe her! This means that to love Mary as God wishes us to love her and as she merits to be loved, we must love her with the fervent love of the Heart of Jesus Himself.

It is precisely here that the beautiful and sublime practice of the total consecration to Mary finds its rightful place of honor. Out of love for souls and through His love for Mary, the eldest daughter of the Father, the King Jesus stripped Himself of His majesty in her womb, becoming her own child, her captive, for nine months before Bethlehem and for thirty years at Nazareth. Therein lies the measure of our love for Mary: total dependence through complete and loving surrender of our entire being to her maternal Heart.

To exchange our life for hers, means to live dependent upon her, as the Infant-God was nourished by her, in so doing we surrender all our personal interests and good, present and future, provided that the Reign of Mary be the certain dawn of the Reign of the Heart of Jesus. In this sense *"I am all yours, O Virgin Mary!"*

One final thought. What have I not received from Jesus? Yet everything has been given to me through the mediation of Mary!

Well, by offering myself to the Queen of love, it is my wish, in union with Jesus, to pay my great debt of gratitude to Mary. Jesus loves Mary with a grateful love, for she it was who gave Him the power of suffering, of agonizing and of dying, of becoming our Savior by the shedding of His Blood on the cross, of being our priest and victim, of being our own very brother. This capacity of lowliness and of mortality was assumed by the Word in the womb of the Virgin Mary. And there it was that through Him and in Him she prepared that most excellent gift, the royal unction of our priesthood.

To repay this munificence of the Queen adequately, I want, as St. John Eudes said, "to make the Lord grow" in my soul unto the fullness of the age of Christ, sanctifying myself and thus becoming more and more a son and a priest of Mary. Next I want Him to "grow" in the souls He has committed to my care and whom, in turn, I entrust to the Queen of Apostles. Lastly, I wish to glorify Mary in order to repay, in union with Jesus my eldest Brother the incomparable, the unique glory with which the Queen has crowned for eternity both Jesus Christ, her firstborn,* and — in Him and with Him — us, the "younger brothers," priests of Mary, Queen of our priestly hearts.

"To the Sacred Hearts of Jesus and Mary, honor, love, and glory!"

---

*A few lines above Father Mateo explained in what sense Mary has crowned Jesus. The Son of God owes to His mother His humanity and His power of suffering and dying, of being a **priest** and **victim**. In this sense Jesus is indebted to her for His Priesthood.

Act of Consecration to the Justice of Christ the Adorable Judge

I know whom I trust! My Judge as well as my Saviour! Through Him, and with Him, and in Him, is to Thee, God the Father Almighty, in the Unity of the Holy Ghost, all honor and glory! (three times)

To the Heart of the eternal Father and for the glory of the most holy Paraclete, for the honor of the most august, most adorable Trinity, Father, Son, and Holy Ghost, I offer up my whole life with all my shortcomings.

Furthermore, in advance, I lovingly consecrate my agony and my death to Christ, my Judge and my Lord, in a spirit of perfect contrition and humility, as well as confident love and thanksgiving. So may it be!

Mother of fair love and mercy; Queen of the Cenacle and priests, Mediatrix of all graces, pray for me, now and at the hour of my death.

Saint Joseph, comfort and help me, I beseech thee in my last hour. Amen.

My own dearest sister, Little Thérèse, obtain from the Father that I may live and die in perfect charity.

Guardian Angel, my beloved brother, I trust in thee, help me!

To Christ, the Son of God, the most equitable Judge, be honor, praise, love, and glory in the unity of the Father and the Paraclete. Amen.

✝

I believe that the Father judges no one, but that He reserves to His Son our judgment, and to Him alone belongs all power and true sanction.

I believe with the most steadfast faith in the infinite justice of Christ, my adorable judge.

I believe that He alone has the power to destroy my body and to sentence my soul to the eternal flames of hell.

If, then, love be the fulfillment of the Law, love for our Lord would not be true love unless I feared to offend the Lord and thereby to be deprived of God for an eternity of damnation. Hence, "the fear of the Lord is the beginning of wisdom."

✝

Therefore, because I must and want to love God with all my heart, with all my soul, and with all my mind, I fear Jesus my Judge, but I fear Him with a filial fear, that is, with a fear suffused with love.

I fear indeed so that I may be able to love with a strong love for all eternity.

I fear the holiness of the Lord!

I fear the most just anger of the Lord!

I fear the adorable vengeance of the Lord!

I fear the irrevocable sentence of the Lord!

Grant, O Lord, that I may have a constant fear as well as love of Thy holy name.

I fear my most sweet Saviour in the crib in Bethlehem and I love my Judge coming in the clouds of heaven in majesty and glory; grant that both may find me prepared.

I fear Jesus my Judge because I have sinned exceedingly in thought, word, and deed, sins of ignorance and frailty, but especially sins of malice and ingratitude – have mercy on me!

✝

Indeed, I fear my adorable Judge because I am a sinner, and I know that God's holiness cannot leave sin unpunished nor tolerate it to remain without reparation.

Jesus, Jesus, Judge most just, give to my eyes, I beseech Thee, a fountain of tears, and mixing them in the chalice with Thy Most Precious Blood, cleanse me yet more and redeem me.

†

I groan and tremble like one guilty, because – even though today, aided by the mercy and grace of God, I have good will – I humbly recognize my inconstancy and I fear my changeableness.

†

O God, come to my aid! O King of love, make haste to help me, have mercy on me!

O Christ, Judge of the living and the dead, most just and most wise, I love Thee! O Christ, Judge, most faithful and almighty,

I praise Thee! O Christ, Judge, truthful and omniscient,

I glorify Thee! O Christ, Judge, ineffable and infallible,

I adore Thee! O Christ, Judge, I fear Thee, for

Thou alone art holy – Holiness itself!

Jesus, Jesus, most just, prostrate before Thee, I beseech Thee for the glory of the Father and the Paraclete, through Mary, thy most tender mother and my mother, do not forsake me in that dreadful day of judgment, do not cast me into everlasting fire.

Be my Saviour, not only my Judge, O Lord!

For the glory of the Father and the Paraclete, and for Thy glory, number me among the blessed and save me!

†

Yes, through the love of the Father, through the grace of the Paraclete, through the tenderness of the Mother of Sorrows, Jesus, Jesus, most just and most meek Judge, Thou who knowest all things, Thou who searchest the hearts and minds of men, turn Thy face from my sins, and do not take Thy Holy Spirit from me.

Jesus, Jesus, King and Saviour, Mediator and Victim, Jesus most just Judge, blot out all my faults, before I am called to stand before Thy tribunal to give an account of my stewardship.

I know whom I trust. I am certain that Thou, Lord Jesus, art able to preserve until that day of Thy visitation, when Thou shalt come to judge, the trust which Thou hast committed to me.

In that day of might, show me the Father and it will be sufficient.

Come, Lord Jesus, come and kindly grant me, not because of my merits, but because of Thy forgiveness and mercy, the crown promised to Thy most unworthy, yet penitent and confident servant, namely, Thy great glory and Thy love.

I will love Thee for all eternity with all my heart, with all my soul, and with all my mind.

Jesus, Jesus, grant that in that supreme hour I may be able to say to Thee, with St. Bonaventure, these words of confidence, of friendship, and of peace:

I have found the Heart of a King, I have found the Heart of a Brother, I have found the Heart of a Friend, most kind Jesus! Oh, how good it is, how pleasing it is, to dwell and to die in this Heart. It is good for me to be here forever.

I know whom I trust!

In Thy Heart, Jesus, most just Judge, I commend my heart to Thee. In Thy Hands, Saviour King and Judge, I commend my heart to Thee. In Thy Hands, Saviour King and Judge, I commend my spirit to the Father.

Through Him, and with Him, and in Him, is to Thee, God the Father Almighty, in the Unity of the Holy Ghost, all honor and glory!

Salve Regina... Confiteor...

Act of Consecration
to the Three Persons
of the Blessed Trinity

To the Father

Abba, Abba, per Ipsum et cum Ipso et in Ipso, I consecrate my whole being to You, Creator and Father, whose omnipotence drew me from nothing through love and only through love.

Abba, Abba, Adonai, God of glory and majesty, I adore You with my heart and my mind.

Honor, praise and love to the eternal and beloved Father!

Abba, Abba, Jehovah, God of mercy and charity, I adore You with my heart and my mind.

Honor, praise and love to the eternal and beloved Father!

Abba, Abba, Elohim, God of wisdom and justice, I adore You with my heart and my mind.

Honor, praise and love to the eternal and beloved Father!

Adonai, Jehovah, Elohim, I adore and love You with Israel and the Church; with Abraham, Isaac, Jacob; with heaven, purgatory and earth.

Abba, Abba, per Ipsum et cum Ipso et in Ipso, I offer You an infinite thanksgiving for the gift of the Word, Thy Son, my Saviour, my Judge, my adorable Friend.

Abba, Abba, per Jpsum et cum Ipso et in Ipso, I offer You a perfect reparation for my sins. I beg pardon for them all, especially for the sin of ingratitude.

Parce, Pater adorande et dilectissime. Parce, Abba et miserere.

Abba, Abba, per Ipsum et cum Ipso et in Ipso, I abandon myself filially in life and in death to You, to Your Fatherly Heart, asking only for one grace: to love You, Abba, toto corde, tota anima, tota mente for all eternity.

To the Merciful Love
of the Sacred Heart

Per Ipsum et cum Ipso et in Ipso, I consecrate myself to Your Sacred Heart, as through Your own adorable Hands You gave Yourself to me on Holy Thursday.

With the simplicity of the Little Flower;

with the seraphic flame of St. Francis of Assisi;

with the apostolic fire of St. Francis Xavier;

with the perfect abandonment of St. Margaret Mary,

I deliver myself in life and in death, as a Christian, as a religious, and as a priest, with all the graces of my triple vocation, but also with all the shortcomings and sins of my life.

Yes, I consecrate myself to the infinite and merciful love of the Sacred Heart of Jesus: diligam Te Domfne, toto corde, tota am'ma, tota mente.

And so that my oblation may be acceptable to the Father and for the glory of the Blessed Trinity, I offer it in the wound of the pierced side of my Saviour, the Victim of my daily Mass. I present it in the Precious Blood of my chalice.

And to render it less unworthy of the adorable King, I ask the Mother of fair love to offer this, my poor gift, in her Immaculate and Sorrowful Heart, for the glory of the Father and the Son and the Holy Ghost.

Through this consecration I intend to give thanks most especially for the ineffable gift of my priesthood and for the miracle of love of my daily Mass.

With my hands in the hands of the Immaculate Queen I promise to make the greatest effort to be a saint at the altar for the glory of the Blessed Trinity and the redemption of many priestly souls.

It is my explicit will to renew this consecration to the merciful Love of the Sacred Heart every morning during Holy Mass, humbly imploring the supreme grace of being, in time and in eternity, a saintly priest of the Blessed Trinity, and of Mary, the Immaculate and Sorrowful Queen, through a thrice holy daily Mass.

TO THE PARACLETE

Per Ipsum et cum Ipso et in Ipso, I consecrate myself to the Holy Ghost, substantial Light and Love; to the Paraclete sent by the Father to crown the work of Christ the Redeemer.

Holy Ghost, I adore You, in the Sacred Heart of the Man-God, and of the supreme and adorable Priest, created through Your inspiration in the womb of the Virgin Mary.

I adore You, O Paraclete, whose omnipotent breathing created the Christian Church in the Cenacle on Pentecost Sunday.

Accept, O Holy Ghost, the gift of my soul, of my heart and of my body, and transform my whole life into Yours for the glory of the Blessed Trinity.

Come, O Paraclete, come with Your sevenfold gifts and sanctify me.

Adorable Paraclete, in a special way I consecrate to You my priesthood.

O, infinite thanks for my priestly character!

Infinite thanks for my priestly powers!

Infinite thanks for my priestly saving mission!

O, infinite thanks particularly for the ineffable treasure of the Holy Sacrifice of the Mass!

As a proof that You deign to accept me, may my daily Mass, by Your grace, be really and truly a hymn of praise and glory to the Blessed Trinity, whose solemn feast I wish to celebrate every morning at the altar cum omni militia coelesti, that through You, O Paraclete, I may really be, in life and death, an Alter Chiistus.

Gloria Patri flagranti amore Filii; inflamma cor meum amore Filii!

Gloria Filio flagranti amore Patris, inflamma cor meum amore Patris!

Gloria Spiritui Sancto flagranti amore Patris et Filii: inflamma cor meum amore Patris et Filii et amore Tuo!

Per Te sciamus, da Patrem Noscamus atque Filium, Teque utriusque Spiritum Credamus omni tempore.

Oremus: Deus, qui corda fidelium Sancti Spiritus illustiatione docuisti, da nobis in eodem Spiiitu recta sapere; et de eius semper consolatione gaudere. Per Christum Dominum Nostrum. Amen.

Consecration of Priests to the Sacred Heart of Jesus

Sacred Heart of Jesus, King of love, through the Immaculate Heart of Mary, Queen of the Clergy and Queen of Apostles, I consecrate forever to Your merciful love, my heart, my soul, and all my undertakings.

Adorable Friend of priests, ever faithful to Your promises, I entrust to You the work of my sanctification. Help me to become a saint. Grant me the grace to bring to You many souls, even those most hardened by sin, according to the promise You explicitly made to St. Margaret Mary.

O merciful Heart of Jesus, in order that I may love You with my whole heart, with my whole soul and with all my strength, and so that I may really make You better known and better loved, keep me in the wound of Your sacred side, and grant that, burning with love for You, I may dwell there in time and for eternity. Amen

DOCTRINAL PRACTICES PROPOSED BY FATHER MATEO

LITTLE CHAPLET OF THE PARACLETE

As proposed by Father Mateo, SS.CC

It is sad to realize, and indeed only too true, that the Holy Spirit does not play a prominent role in the spiritual life of most Christians. Those who have genuine devotion to Him are few and far between.

This is, undoubtedly, a great defect in our spiritual life. We are thereby deficient in understanding and holiness.

Let us react! It is never too late! Here is a practical way to honor the Holy Spirit and draw His sevenfold gifts upon us.

In the very first place, let us try to spread this doctrinal devotion, love for the Paraclete, suitable for the highest spiritual aspirations of the best among our Catholic people, and let us form the praiseworthy habit of reciting this chaplet as a homage to the Holy Spirit.

Come, Holy Spirit, enlighten my mind! Come, inflame my heart!

Method of Reciting

1. Take your Rosary and recite the Apostles' Creed.

2. After the Creed, *very slowly and devoutly say the* Glory be to the Father.

3. Then say the Our Father.

4. Now, very fervently, say this ejaculation:

Father, Father, send us the promised Paraclete, through Jesus Christ our Lord. Amen.

5. On each bead, instead of the Hail Mary, *say with a burning heart:*

Come, Holy Spirit, fill the hearts of Thy faithful and kindle in them the fire of Thy love!

6. After the tenth bead recite the following official prayer:

Send forth Thy Spirit and they shall be created. And Thou shalt renew the face of the earth.

Let us Pray

O God, who didst instruct the hearts of Thy faithful by the light of the Holy Spirit, grant us by the same Spirit to be truly wise and evermore to rejoice in His consolation. Through Christ our Lord. Amen.

7. Then recite the second decade and all the others in the same way as explained (beginning at number 3): Our Father, *etc....*

After the seventh and last decade, recite the Hail, Holy Queen *in honor of the Blessed Virgin, our Heavenly Queen, who presided in the Cenacle on the great Sunday of Pentecost.*

Suggested Reflections

A few short reflections may be made on the seven glorious mysteries relating to the seven wonderful operations of the Paraclete. These meditations should be made briefly, between each decade.

FIRST MYSTERY: Let us honor the Holy Spirit and adore Him who is Substantial Love, proceeding from the Father and the Son, and uniting Them in infinite and eternal love.

SECOND MYSTERY: Let us honor the operation of the Holy Spirit and adore Him in the Immaculate Conception of Mary, sanctifying her from the first moment with the fullness of grace.

THIRD MYSTERY: Let us honor the operation of the Holy Spirit and adore Him in the Incarnation of the Word, the Son of God by His Divine nature, and the Son of the Virgin by the flesh.

FOURTH MYSTERY: Let us honor the operation of the Holy Spirit and adore Him in the promulgation of the Church on the glorious day of Pentecost.

FIFTH MYSTERY: Let us honor the operation of the Holy Spirit and adore Him dwelling in the Church and assisting her faithfully according to the Divine promise, even to the consummation of the world.

SIXTH MYSTERY: Let us honor the wonderful operation of the Holy Spirit within the Church, creating other Christs, the priests, and bestowing the fullness of the priesthood on the bishops.

SEVENTH MYSTERY: Let us honor the operation of the Holy Spirit, the adorable Sanctifier, and adore Him in His hidden and marvelous work of the formation of saints in the Church.

PRACTICES

Recite this little chaplet often, especially on Sundays, even every day.

Recite it: when some important decision must be made and when special help is needed; every day during recollections and retreats; as a preparation for the Feast of Pentecost.

This simple chaplet must become a familiar practice and one of our great Catholic devotions: We must have enlightened piety. The Blessed Virgin, Queen of Apostles and of the Cenacle, will bless you. You will thus win her heart "full of grace," for she is the masterpiece of the Holy Spirit's operation. In your devotions always keep in mind the essential. The first of all devotions must be to the Blessed Trinity, which of necessity includes the Holy Spirit.

THE MASS OF SAINT JOHN

In keeping with his strong preaching on the "greatest of all doctrinal devotions," that of the Holy Sacrifice of the Mass, Father Mateo has promulgated far and wide what he calls "the Mass of St. John." It is not a new idea for it simply encourages Catholics to unite themselves frequently with the Mass being celebrated uninterruptedly throughout the world.

The title brings out the fact that this practice consists of the three essential parts of the Holy Sacrifice, namely, the Offertory, the Consecration and the Communion. Holy Mass as celebrated by St. John was much shorter than our present Mass formula, yet consisted of these three elements. Hence the title, "Mass of St. John."

It is particularly appealing to priests as it stresses the priestly practice of keeping oneself frequently united with the Holy Sacrifice. Here is an excellent and practical means of "living the Mass" in daily life. It is especially helpful on the occasion of a priest's private Holy Hour or visits to the Blessed Sacrament.

For the glory of the Blessed Trinity, In union with all the priests in the Church offering the Holy Sacrifice, I unite myself to them, Per Ipsum, et cum Ipso et in Ipso.

I

Receive, O holy Father, almighty and eternal God, this spotless host, which I, Thy unworthy servant, offer unto Thee, my living and true God, for mine own countless sins, offenses and negligences, and for all here present; as also for all faithful Christians living and dead, that it may avail both for my own and their salvation unto life eternal. Amen.

We offer unto Thee, O Lord, the chalice of salvation, beseeching Thy clemency, that it may ascend in the sight of Thy divine majesty with a sweet savor, for our own salvation and for that of the whole world. Amen.

II

The day before He suffered He took bread into His holy and venerable hands, and with His eyes lifted up to heaven, unto Thee, God, His almighty Father, giving thanks to Thee, He blessed, broke and gave it to His disciples, saying: Take and eat ye all of this,

FOR THIS IS MY BODY

In like manner, after He had supped, taking also this excellent chalice into His holy and venerable hands, and giving thanks to Thee, He blessed and gave it to His disciples, saying: Take and drink ye all of this,

FOR THIS IS THE CHALICE OF MY BLOOD, OF THE NEW AND ETERNAL TESTAMENT: THE MYSTERY OF FAITH: WHICH SHALL BE SHED FOR YOU AND FOR MANY UNTO THE REMISSION OF SINS.

As often as ye shall do these things, ye shall do them in remembrance of Me.

III

Lord, I am not worthy that Thou shouldst enter under my roof; say but the word and my soul shall be healed. *(3 times)*

May the Body of our Lord Jesus Christ preserve my soul to life everlasting. Amen.

May the Blood of our Lord Jesus Christ preserve my soul to life everlasting. Amen.

Here make a spiritual Communion

Useful Prayers

Lord Jesus, who art our most loving Redeemer and a Priest forever, look mercifully on us, Thy humble suppliants, whom Thou hast been pleased to call Thy friends and partakers of Thy priesthood. We are Thine; we wish to be Thine forever: therefore to Thy Most Sacred Heart which Thou hast shown to oppressed humanity as their only safe refuge, we dedicate and devote ourselves wholly this day. Thou who hast promised plenteous fruit in the divine ministry to those priests who are devoted to Thy Sacred Heart, make us, we beseech Thee, fit workmen in Thy vineyard, truly meek and humble, filled with the spirit of devotion and patience, so fired with love of Thee that we shall never cease to enkindle and quicken the same fire of love in the hearts of the faithful. Renew our hearts, therefore, in the fire of Thy Heart, so that henceforth we shall desire nothing save to promote Thy glory and to win for Thee the souls whom Thou didst redeem by Thy Precious Blood. Show Thy mercy, good Shepherd, chiefly to those priests, our brethren, if there be any such, who, walking in the vanity of sense, have saddened Thee and Thy beloved Spouse, Holy Church, by their lamentable falling away from Thee. Grant us grace to bring them back to Thy embrace, or, at least, to atone for their crimes, to repair the harm they have done, and to lessen the sorrow they have caused Thee, by the consolation of our love. Allow each one of us, finally, to pray to Thee in the words of Saint Augustine: "O sweet Jesus, live Thou in me, and let the living coal of Thy love burn brightly in my spirit, and grow into a perfect conflagration; let it burn perpetually on the altar of my heart, let it glow in my marrow, let it blaze up in the most secret places of my soul; in the day of my consummation let me be found totally consumed thereby in Thy presence, who with the Father and the Holy Ghost livest and reignest one God for ever and ever, Amen." (*Raccolta, no. 744*)

A Prayer to Stir Up
the Grace of the Priesthood

Dearest Jesus, who of Thy great goodness hast called me to be Thy follower in preference to countless others and hast raised me to the high dignity of Thy priesthood, bestow upon me abundantly, I pray, Thy divine help in fulfilling my duties in a right spirit. I beseech Thee, Lord Jesus, to stir up in me Thy grace both today and always, that grace which is in me by reason of the laying on of hands of the bishop. O mighty Physician of souls, heal me in such wise that I may never be entangled in sinful habits, but that I may renounce them all and be enabled to please Thee even to the day of my death. Amen. (*Raccolta, 733*)

A Prayer for the Grace of
Preaching Holily and Fruitfully

Give me, O Lord, a mild and judicious eloquence which shall keep me from being puffed up and exalted above my brethren by reason of Thy gifts. Put into my mouth, I beseech Thee, words of consolation and edification and exhortation through Thy Holy Spirit, that I may be enabled to exhort the good to better things, and, by word and example, to recall to the straight way of Thy righteousness those who walk perversely. Let the words which Thou shalt give Thy servant, be like to sharp javelins and burning arrows that shall pierce and enkindle unto Thy fear and holy love the minds of all them that hear me. Amen. (*St. Anselm, Bishop, Confessor and Doctor*) (*Raccolta, no. 738*)

PRAYERS FOR HOLINESS OF LIFE

O good Jesu, grant that I may be a priest after Thine own Heart. (*Raccolta, no. 739*)

Almighty and merciful God, graciously attend to my humble prayers; and make me, Thy servant, whom Thou hast appointed to dispense Thy heavenly mysteries, through no merits of mine own, but only of the infinite bounty of Thy mercy, a worthy minister at Thy sacred altar, that what is set forth by my voice, may be confirmed by Thy hallowing grace. Through Christ our Lord. Amen. (*Roman Missal*) (*Raccolta, no. 740*)

O Almighty God, let Thy grace assist us, that we who have undertaken the office of Priesthood, may be able to wait upon Thee worthily and devoutly, in all purity, and with a good conscience. And if we cannot live in so great innocency of life as we ought to do, grant to us at least worthily to lament the sins that we have committed; and in the spirit of humility, and with the full purpose of a good will, to serve Thee more earnestly for the time to come. Through Christ our Lord. Amen. (*The Imitation of Christ, Book IV, Ch. xi, n. 7*) (*Raccolta, no. 741*)

www.ingramcontent.com/pod-product-compliance
Lightning Source LLC
Chambersburg PA
CBHW021101090426
42738CB00006B/448